Zillennial
Panic
The Dreams and Ramblings
of an Artistic Failure
K. Weary

ISBN 979-8-9864240-8-8 (Print)

ISBN 979-8-9864240-9-5 (Ebook)

Illustrations and cover design by K. Weary

Published by V&KPublishing

kwearybooks@gmail.com

vandkpublishing.com

-

This book is for me.

It is my pain and my joy, my stories and my words from a hundred different versions of myself. It is a reminder that I exist and that I change and that I don't.

-

But this book is also for you.

For what is poetry but shouting into the void, "I am full, I am broken, I am human!" And hoping to hear an answer, hoping you are not alone.

-

-

Contents

Foreward

I don't know exactly what makes me want to publish these poems - this story. If you do not know me now, you will know me by the end of this book - you will know me a degree more than my own mother. But you, dear reader, will still be a stranger to me.

I think I am ok with this. I am burdened by the common curse of an eldest daughter to constantly seek outside approval, and yet never to trust it. I hope you will like my poems, but that is not why I am publishing them.

I think it is enough for me to know that you are human, and to hope you may find some comfort in the universal nature of my feelings - if not my experiences. This way, we hold each other as if we were friends, leaning against one another on the couch. We are not looking at each other, but looking forward.

In case you would still prefer to know me before getting a little tour of my innermost thoughts, let me introduce myself.

My name I will not give you, at least not in full. Call me K. I am both an artist and a scientist by nature, but a teacher by trade. I was homeschooled in the rural midwest in a post 9-11 America by Christian conservative parents, only one of whom I believe truly does try to love me.

I have been other places in the world and loved them, but I have only lived here - and I do not see myself leaving. The primary reason for this is that I am a creature of habit, but also that my soul is anchored to the few points of light in this wasteland that are the people I love most fiercely in the world.

That is another thing. Contrary to what you must imagine of a poet, I have never been in love. Not in the Hollywood sense anyway. But here is not the place to discuss my spot on the asexuality spectrum nor the disdain I have for the overwhelming amount of media that lauds romantic love above all else.

I believe - or wish to believe - through one of the longest lasting good things in my life, in platonic soulmates. Please do not extrapolate from this that I am part of some tragic one-sided romance. I am not.

I need not add tragedy to my story, as tame as it is. It is enough to live in the time that we do, in the place that we do, and to feel the hopelessness and helplessness that comes with it. I have it good overall, but that does not stop this book from existing.

The poet at the beginning of this book is a child. She is a product of Iowa's fertile soil - planted right alongside the corn and the racism and the religious absolutism and the loneliness. I hope you can forgive her for that.

The poet at the end of this book is a queer, neurodivergent, schoolteacher who's finally learning to love herself.

Have I gone on long enough? Do you feel as if you know me? Do you think we could be friends? Do you feel your shoulder pressed into mine like the solid, uncomplicated weight of understanding? Do you hear my voice crack over some of the words? Do you hear the rage when I read others? Do you hear me scream? Do you feel and hear the laughter that we share to diffuse the tension of sorrow?

I will welcome you here where I have shut out others, if only because there may be some of you (some of you like me) who need every so often to be welcomed.

Now, come close to me. And listen.

-K. Weary

- The Early Years -

2007

(Innocence)

The simple rhymes of a child discovering language as an avenue for wonder.

Age: 10

Kittens

- Wonder at fragility and care (their mother cares for me better than my own.)

A kitten starts out small. It cannot see or hear,

They meow and they meow,

'Til their mother is near.

When they open their eyes,

They can hardly believe,

All the things they can see.

As they get older, they jump and they leap,

And when they're done, they collapse in a heap.

Books

- The poorly constructed lines of a child whose friends were ideas.

Books are my favorite thing.

When I read them I feel as though I could sing.

There are books that have adventure or mystery.

Some of the books have excitement or history.

No matter what kind of book

Chances are I'll take a look.

Now you've read about me,

You know my favorite place is the library.

Now the last thing I'm going to say is hard to say,

So, I'll say it this way.

Whatever kind of book, no matter what shape or size,

Each one is special, now I usually don't tell lies.

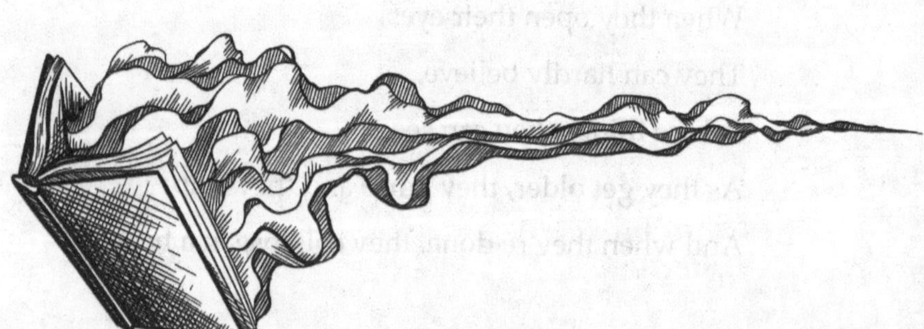

A Spider

- Awe at nature and justice for the unwanted. Here I see parts of myself that have not changed. (Spiders never could scare me as much as people)

A little spider
Climbing up
A tree.

I thought
That little
Spider must
Be glad
To be free.

My other
Friends think
To smash it.

They think it is
Right.

2011 (Rediscovery)

I remember poetry is a thing I can do. I try more diligently for proper lines to express once again my love for the natural world - my escape.

Age: 14

Birds

- I don't remember what my mother said about this one. I only remember being disappointed.

Birds, wonderful, beautiful things,

Birds, like paintings with wings.

Swooping and diving, flapping and soaring,

Perching and pecking, it never gets boring.

Masters of aerodynamics and lift,

Human pilots wish they had such a gift.

Eating bugs and other nasty pests,
Busy, but singing, making their nests.

Shrilling and chirping and tweeting,
Singing, while they do their eating.

The very last thing that I wish to see,
Is how the world would be,
Without birds.

The Monarch

- I hatched a monarch and she wasn't afraid of me. I doubt anything else could have given me that euphoria.

We call her a monarch, rightly so, for she's a queen.

A butterfly more royal in blood, you will never have seen.

Her manners are exquisite, she sips nectar from a blossom.

Graceful in everything, her flying skills are awesome.

Her royal robes are of striking orange and ebony black,

White spots adorn the edges, as well as on her back.

Her beauty surpasses all who dare to challenge she,

None can match her coloration, form, and symmetry.

Her throne is different each time she rests.

She sits on beautiful flowers, and sits on only the best.

No servants has she, for she's quite self-sufficient.

Most queens are lazy but this one is different.

A crown is lacking on her head (even though a few
would heed it)

She does not wear one for, simply, she does not need it.

She is a monarch of the sky, and it's most clear to me,

She is the least honored and most beloved queen.

Dandelion Fluff

- The cycles and inherit sorrow of nature. I sat in a boxelder tree, watching the wind on an unmowed lawn, while my friends went on without me.

Dandelion fluff,

Dandelion fair,

Dandelion puff,

In her soft, fluffy hair.

She loses her seeds,

With every wind gust.

She loses more seeds,

And lose them she must.

She loses her seeds,

For hours and hours.

She loses the seeds,

So that they'll become flowers.

Kissing them goodbye
As she watches each go,
Dispersing a love on them
That they'll never know.

By early morning light,
The dandelion's bare.
No yellow petals,
No fluffy hair.

She smiles and thinks
Of each little seed.
Dispersing them was her last
And most important deed.

Standing on the edge of self-disclosure, chained by rhyme.

Age: 15

Fjord

- I just think this one's funny.

The coast of Norway

Has been bored.

By a glacier,

It's been cored,

With many long harbors,

Each called a fjord.

Without these cuts,

It would look like a gourd.

Spring Storm
- This one still rings true.

When the weather seems to be turning warm,
Always comes the cold spring storm.

We thought it'd be nice, but instead,
Winter rears its ugly head.

All at once the world turns white,
And all the creatures run in fright.

All the while I sit cozy inside,
Needing nowhere to run and hide.

Watching as the snow covers the tree,
Thinking of rhymes for my poetry.

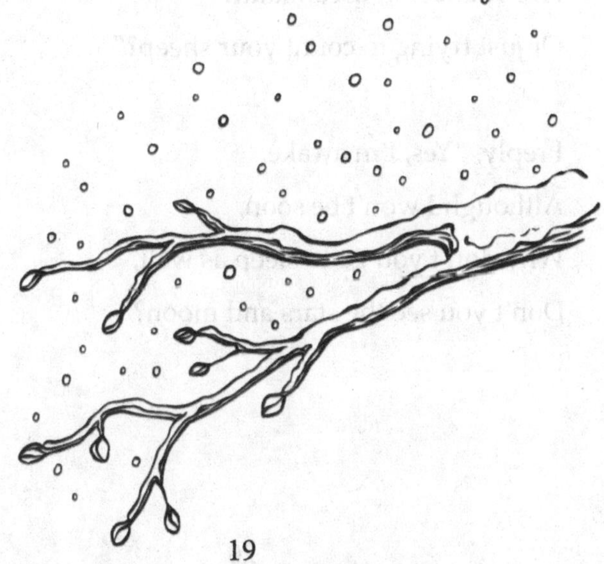

My Sister's Second Wind

- One of the only truly lighthearted things I've made. She inspires that in me - we do that for each other.

My eyes begin to close,

As I'm lying in my bed,

The memories of the ending day,

Swirling in my head.

About this time some nights,

Although she was tired before,

My sister gets her second wind,

And then, well, she isn't anymore.

My younger sister says to me,

"Hey are you asleep?

Are you lost in dreamland?

Or just trying to count your sheep?"

I reply, "Yes, I'm awake,

Although I won't be soon,

Why don't you go to sleep as well,

Don't you see the stars and moon?"

"Yes, I can see them shining there,
But I can't fall asleep,
Maybe in a little while I'll
Fall into oblivion deep.

I'm tired and worn from the day's heat,
And I wish I could close my eyes tight.
But I cannot quell this energy,
Though I try with all my might."

She continues to talk to me,
Way past bedtime in the night,
Until she runs out of things to say,
And reaches to turn off her light.

I love my sister, yes, it's true,
Second wind or not,
But I still sigh when I'm trying to sleep,
And she's complaining that she's hot.

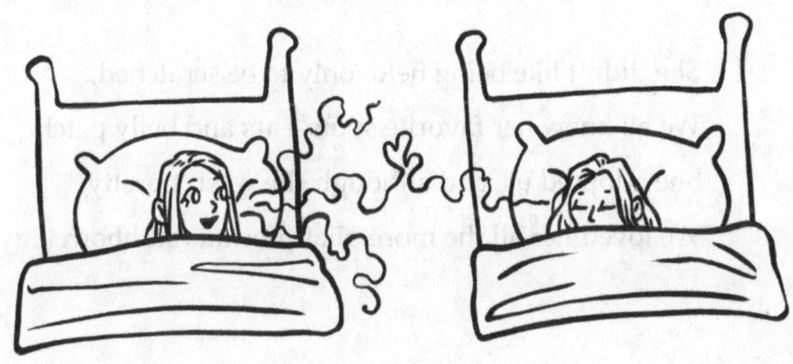

Our Cat Midnight

- Nothing quite as raw as a child grieving over a pet for the first time - I memorialize them in words even now.

Our cat Midnight is a kitty to remember,

And I never thought she wouldn't make it to September.

On August 27th she was buried beneath a tree,

And I pay my final tribute with the following poetry.

Away from a fight Midnight would never shy,

Fearless fighter with a battle-scarred eye.

She was queen of the farm to her last day.

Though new cats would come, none took her place away.

When we needed a laugh we'd just go to this cat,

With her peach fuzz tummy which was very fat.

We called her smudge pot, she was black and quite round,

When we poured out the food, she just went to town.

She didn't like being held, only to be scratched,

We all knew her favorite spots, ears and belly patch.

She adopted us, and although she wasn't pretty,

We loved her all the more, that precious stubborn kitty.

She was one tough cookie, worn, but still so sweet,

And my life was ever changed, the day she went to sleep.

We loved our cat Midnight to the very last day,

And no other cat can take her memory away.

Chick-a-Dee

- A snapshot.

I grab my camera and snap a picture,

But to no avail,

I can't capture the way you hop about,

Or the way you wiggle your tail.

Circle of Tears

- Found hidden away in my closet like a shameful secret.

My heart starts to hurt as my tears stain the page,

I've locked myself in an emotional cage.

Constantly striving or trying to strive,

I feel so alone and barely alive.

Always exhausting my mind, heart, and soul.

Going, yet never reaching a goal.

Trapped in this place of never ending tears,

Will anyone save me from all of my fear?

I Saw a Gleam

- It was quite the denial from a Good Christian Girl to say I didn't know who I had written this about...I couldn't bring myself salvation.

I saw a gleam of hate in her eye,

When she glanced my way.

I saw a shimmer of bitterness,

A liquid refusal to pray.

A crystallized anger,

A liquidized pain,

A sharp diamond frustration,

From trying to gain.

A gleam of self pity

A sheen unforgiving

A glisten of despair

Mixed with self-living.

A drop of snake's venom

From the curved fangs of pride,

Anger with all

That's held tight inside.

It hung, suspended,
In the wet of her eye,
It hung like a tear,
Threatening to cry.

In a flash of a glance,
I saw her life in her eyes,
I saw all her struggles,
Through her happy disguise.

I saw what she wanted,
But on her own, could not find.
A way of escape,
That she hadn't already tried.

I hope she can find it,
For narrow's the way
To let go of the past,
And look to today.

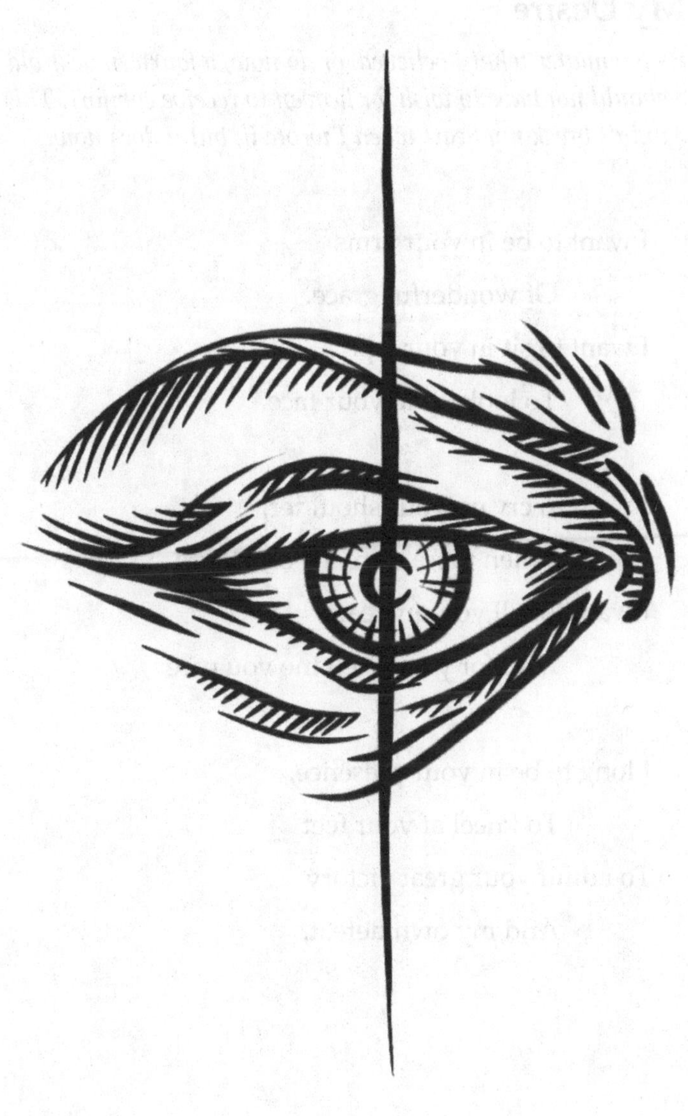

My Desire

*- No matter what I believed, or do now, a fourteen year old girl
should not have to wish for heaven to receive comfort. This
didn't break my heart when I wrote it, but it does now.*

I want to be in your arms

    Of wonderful grace.

I want to sit in your lap.

    To look up at your face.

I want to cry on your shoulder,

    When there's no one else there.

I want to tell you my fears,

    And for you to tell me you care.

I long to be in your presence,

    To kneel at your feet

To admit your great victory

    And my own defeat.

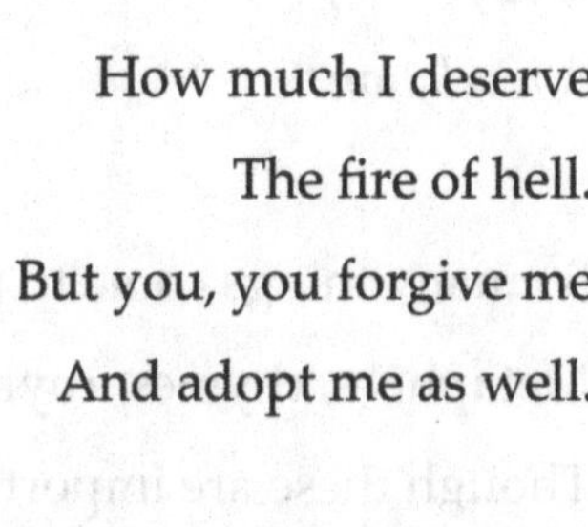

How much I deserve
The fire of hell.
But you, you forgive me
And adopt me as well.

You know my desire,
And you know my worth.
So, please grant me my desire
When I leave this earth.

Poetry

- A revelation.

So many things come to play in poetry.

Metaphors, rhymes, rhythm, and similes.

Though these are important,

(you really must know)

It's putting your feelings,

Into words that will flow.

2013
(Context)

A year of displacement and distraction and despair.

Is this growing up?

Age: 16

Apple Snow

- I start to flirt with figurative language. (Still and always the cycles of nature.)

In time of growth and new life,

When robin young open sky-blue doors,

Come sweet smelling snow,

That does not melt on green floors.

When soft breeze or angel's touch

Send them fluttering down,

Then rest after spinning flight

On dewy, grassy ground.

It comes from heights,

Though not so lofty as the winter stuff.

Fragrant flakes that are warm velvet

Instead of ice-cold fluff.

Turning somersaults as they leave

The trees where they used to room,

What now will become a fruit,

Discards the soft white bloom.

Falling on hands and face

It whispers me a promise true

Snow has fallen, and you will not

See the frost 'til winter blue.

As I feel the damp breeze,

Listen to the whistle of robin and the caw of crow,

I thank God for the spring

And the sun-kissed apple snow.

Faith

*- I wrote so many poems like this, arguing my beliefs to an
invisible voice (I thought that voice was "The World", now I
wonder if it was always just me.)*

You have said to me,

"How do you know God's there?

How do you know he acts?

How do you know he cares?

If I cannot see him

He's not there, Understand?

I cannot believe in things

I can't hold in these hands."

If I can see the plant,

I don't doubt someone sowed the seed,

I know someone wrote the book

If another is to read.

We can't see the sun

In the dark of night,

But we don't doubt it's there,

The moon reflects its light.

If I can hear your voice,

I don't doubt you have a face.

I know that God exists,

From the evidence of his grace.

I see people changing,

I see hard hearts turned,

I see people forgiving,

Instead of giving what's earned.

It's a matter of faith,

Not only what you can see.

I have presented my case,

Maybe someday you'll agree.

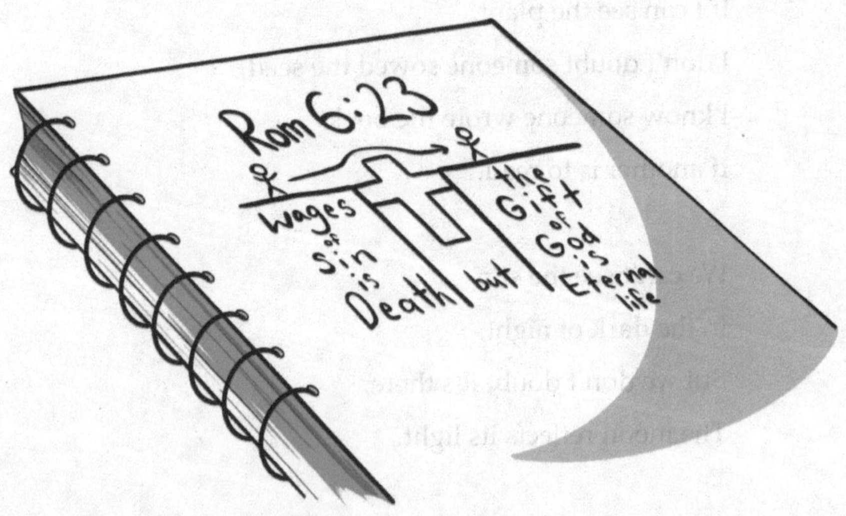

At Iowa Feeders

- A delightful and simple poem that I feel could be a children's book - I wrote it away from its subject, homesick in Arizona.

At Iowa feeders
A congregation of birds,
Arrives to have lunch,
And exchange a few words.

Feather they share,
As well as claw and beak,
But they are all different,
From size, to their speech.

The first bird we'll meet,
Flying high as a kite,
Is proud Mr. Cardinal,
Stretching to his full height.

He may be small,
But he's quite a sight,
With a high crested crown
And crimson coat bright.

Let's not forget Mrs. Cardinal,
That could end in a fight,
Just 'cause she's brown,
Doesn't mean she can't bite.

Bright eyes, and orange beak
That shines in her flight,
She's stunning too,
But camouflaged right.

The birds we'll meet next,
Come in groups, you'll be told,
Come to feed on the thistle,
In bright black and gold.

The gold finch family,
All, young and old,
Are small and they're meek,
But a sight to behold.

Iowa's state bird,
Is the title they hold,
They like Iowa best,
And stick around for the cold.

The next feathered friend,
Our attention to pay,
Is the loud king of the feeder,
Yes, I mean the Blue Jay.

He's big and he's blue,
And he's here to stay.
He's stunning and he knows it,
He shouts his name all the day.

When he calls out his warning
Most heed and fly away.
He will party with friends,
In the treetops they'll play.

The only bird that holds his own,
With this big blue talker,
Is the Red Bellied Woodpecker,
A large, checkered tree stalker.

He's not showy or loud,
He's only a blocker,
He tips his bright red cap
Swinging from his branch rocker.

Though he's very athletic,
He doesn't play soccer,
Upside down you'll see the patch,
That give name to this knocker.

A bundle of energy,
Is the next bird to see,
She's here then she's not,
It's the chick-a-dee-dee.

She leaves then comes back,
Just as quick as can be,
She snaps up a seed,
Then takes it back to her tree.

Her shiny black head,
Is quite hard to see,
As she skips about,
So happy and free.

There are many more birds,
In this feeder city,
But I cannot tell about them all,
I know it's a pity.

But I will tell you these birds,
Whether dull or pretty,
Sing-songish or loud,
Big birds, or bittie,

In big flocks or solitary,
Simpler or neater,
They all belong,
At the Iowa feeders.

Homesick

- This is not a good poem. It is simple and unpolished and melodramatic - but I remember the isolation, the child's desperation and panic, and I sympathize.

If home is where the heart is,

Then I left my heart at home.

It seems to always feel this way,

Whenever I roam.

Home is where the heart is,

And there's a hole inside my chest,

Of all the places I have been,

I think home's the best.

Home is where the heart is,

I can't hear a beat from here.

My heart is much too far away.

And this strange place so near.

Home is where the heart is,

There's only one thing that keeps it beat,

That it won't be too much longer,

Before me and my heart meet.

The Things I've Said

- I thought this was clever (desperate to be heard)

There are things that I've said, that I regret.
There are things I want to say, but I forget.

There are things I wanted to say before,
But after a while I don't anymore.

There are things that I was about to say but did not,
And I wonder what would've happened if I did (a lot).

There are things that I've muttered under my breath,
That, in anger, I wish I could shout out 'til death.

There are things that I've said that I didn't mean.
There are a few things that I've said that are really
keen.

But all the things that I have said soon pass away,
And no one remembers what I said another day.

You Point a Finger

- I begin to dare to accuse my mother on paper.

When I need to cry on your shoulder

You point a finger

When I need you to hold me in your arms

You rationalize

And I'm left with pain in my heart and tears in my
eyes.

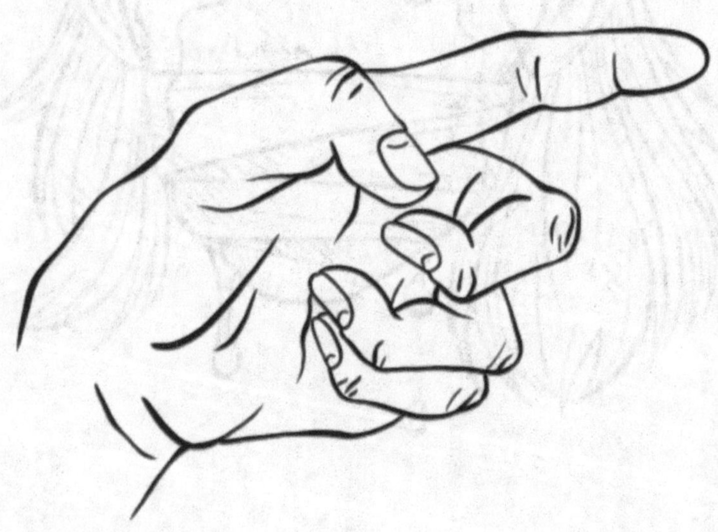

Time

- This is panic.

Time,

The soft ticking of a clock in a quiet room.

Time,

The rush of busy people trying to stay on schedule.

Time,

The still moments when it seems to inch along.

Time,

Busy hours when it seems to disappear.

Time,

To each person is given his share.

Time,

How will you spend yours?

- The Chrysalis -

Wrestling with my own insecurity - it's not too pretty but we all do it.

Age: 17

Fledgling

- A year before graduation and I already start to panic, Mom can't understand why making a phone call is so hard for me.

I have grown too big to fit inside this nest.
I know that to stretch and fly would be best.

But I do not want to leave, I do not want to see,
How far it is below, the safety of this tree.

I am not so sure these oddly colored feathers,

Will be able to let me fly and ward off the weather.

Though now I creep to the edge, I'm dizzied by the
height.

I would love to fly, spread my wings, but I am filled
with fright.

Mother bird makes it look so easy, soaring, singing,
flapping.

But when I start to flap my wings, I find I'd rather be
napping.

I don't know what I'll do once I have gone.

What do birds do when this flying stuff's done?

Should I go build a nest? Search for a mate?

Learn my bird song? Find food for my plate?

If not for you I'd just stay here and worry,

Thanks mother bird for helping me hurry.

I will not fly too far away, once I soar on dull, wobbly
wings,

I hope that you will be proud once I start to sing.

I Am Sure

*- The gospel was never meant to be a tool for me to hurt
myself. The weakness of the rebuttal breaks my heart. (I'm not
sure anymore.)*

The serpent is ever

Whispering inside my ear,

"Are you really sure?

"You and I, and certainly *He*

Knows you have not,

And cannot,

Endure.

"Low undeserving, selfish,

It's clear you are not

really pure."

I shut my ears,

Clutch my Book,

And say,

"You are right...

But I am sure..."

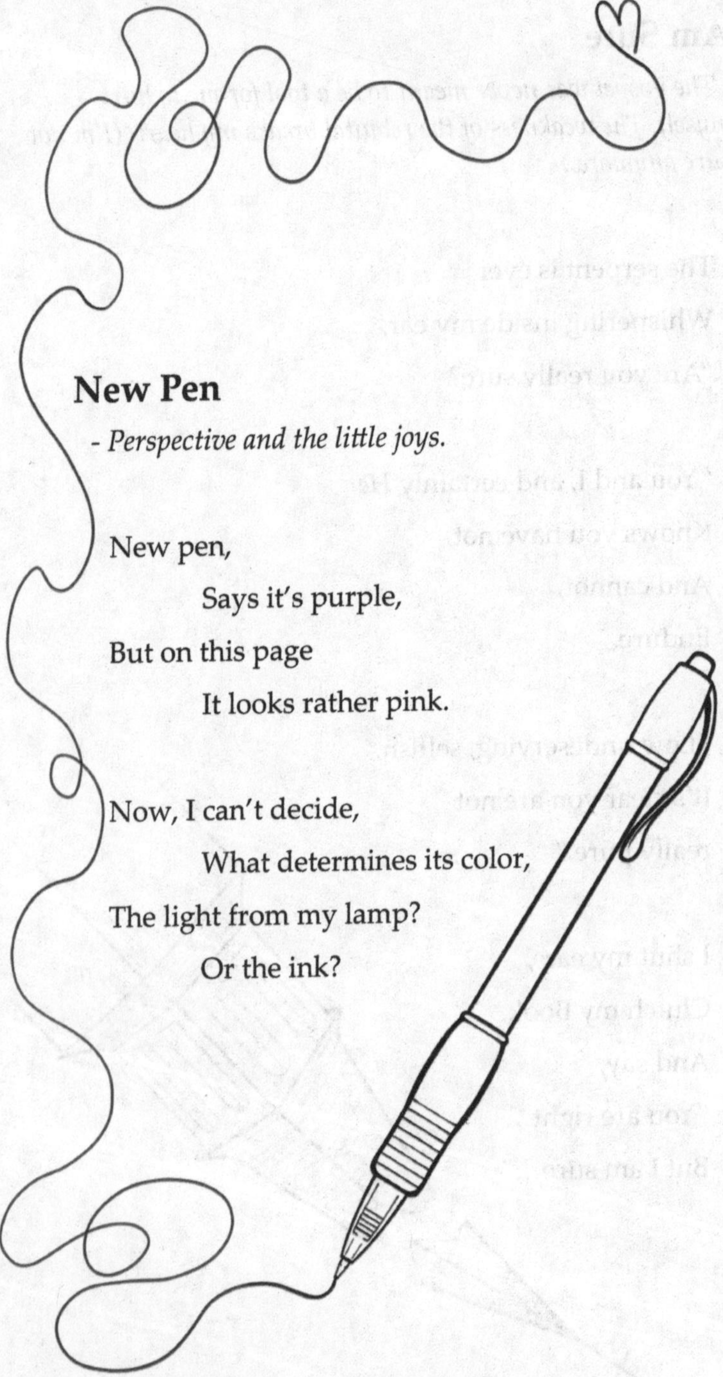

New Pen

- Perspective and the little joys.

New pen,

    Says it's purple,

But on this page

    It looks rather pink.

Now, I can't decide,

    What determines its color,

The light from my lamp?

    Or the ink?

Worth

- This isn't poetry. (Then again when did I promise this was a book of poetry?)

I've never considered myself a flirt, nor will I ever want to be one, it's cruel to toy with others' hearts.

But sometimes – or more than sometimes – I wish at least one person had shown even mildly genuine interest in me.

I know I'm not supposed to draw my value from that, but it would be nice to know that I am desirable.

What is wrong with me? I don't want to be like everyone else, but should the cost of being myself be the loss of anyone wanting me around?

There Was a Heart

- A run-on disaster that proves, once again, I am not as different now as I thought.

There was a heart,

A heart which thrilled at the smallest song of nature or smile from a friend,

a heart which fell with the smallest disapproving glance or tremble of anger,

a heart which stirred easily to frustration and anger yet shied from any confrontation which would reopen wounds that should have turned to scars long ago,

a heart which hated to be wrong and hated the world to think it was right,

a heart which treasured the soft words and smiles of its loved ones inside its deepest treasure chests for the times when it seemed unwanted or unneeded,

(but when those times would come the dusty memories did not seem like enough, for people change)

and the heart had to be reminded that it was doubtful anyone would truly need her like she needed them.

Pews

-I saw demons where there were none, but maybe I was right.

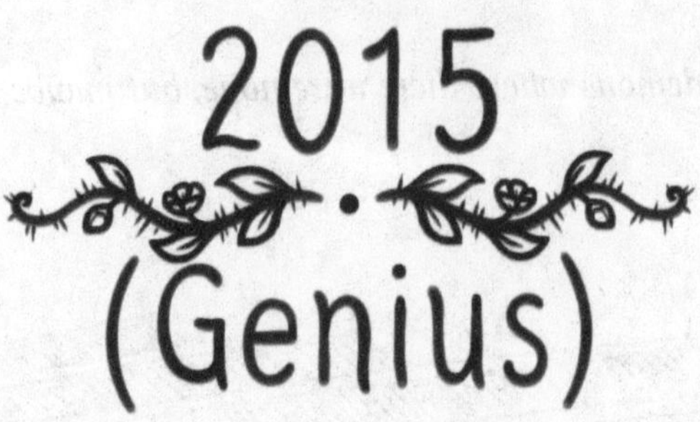

2015
(Genius)

I think myself something greater than I am, and sing songs
into the dark.

Age: 18

Autumn

*- Featured in my book of senior pictures - Mom remembers it
as a poem about trees.*

Blazing triumph of glorious gold

Clouds as smoke curl across the sky

I stand to ponder and behold

And listen to the calling cry

Of birds who wish that they could stay

And wonder at the flaming leaves

But their path leads another way

They sing farewell on laden eaves

But I stand among the leaves and wait
Which crunch and blow across my feet
Finding no path quite clear or straight
Wishing that I could retreat

Wishing things would not change
Missing the warmth of summer's touch
The future, so unsure, frightening, strange
I wonder why I look forward so much

I long for winter's cool, sparkling sleep
Yet crave the delight of memory's spring
But I stand in autumn, with no reason to weep
A fledgling testing her wings.

Don't Play With Fire

- This reads as sexual awakening, but not mine.

Don't play with fire.

It seeps into your bones,

Plays along your skin.

Harmless candles flickering,

When we just begin.

Don't play with fire.

It leaps across carefully laid walls

Ignites your soul,

Becomes a raging inferno,

That will swallow you whole.

Don't play with fire.

It ignites your mind,

Burns behind your eyes,

The searing feeling of fingerprints,

And surprise.

Don't play with fire.

It does not release,

It is beauty, it is death.

It leaves only ash,

Scorches every breath.

Don't play with fire.

Friends

- I yearn for approval from the people around me and break free from verse.

You fill me up, and leave me empty.

You are the most wonderful form of torture,

You make me sing in the depths of my bones.

You make me cry with the ache of an abandoned soul.

Have you ever chosen me?

I don't think so.

I,

Just another traveler beside you.

Destined to leave you.

To be forgotten.

Destined to be forever haunted by your glance,

For a glance, was all you have ever given me.

Yet I cherished those glances,

Hoped against hope that I might mean something to you.

If it was even a fraction of what you mean to me.

I would rejoice.

It is not to be.

I,

Just barely a friend.

Destined to be left at the sidelines,

While the loud ones play.

You play the loudest.

Surrounded by the friends you found so easily.

Have you ever worried you would lose them?

I have worried.

I have worried overmuch.

Have you ever even had to try to make someone like you?

Has it ever bothered you if they don't?

I would doubt it.

You would never guess,

That every gesture,

Every word spoken to me,

Is stored in my mind as precious.

They are my wings.

Destined to let me fall,

With no one to catch me.

Bedside

-I hope you can read backwards.

Human

- I contemplate, perhaps too often, what it is to be human.
(part 1)

Clutching.

Exploring new frontiers simply because they call.

Wondering.

Hoping.

Dreaming about tomorrow.

Crying.

Shouting.

Starving.

Shaking fists at heaven for their own folly.

Loving.

Loving more than self,

> More than life.

> Gazing at the stars.

> Reaching for them.

Clutching and clawing at their breasts for lost love,

> Yet living.

Living

And

Dying

Trying to find a reason to
Live and
To die.

Sitting.
Simply sitting and thinking.
Questioning
Everything.
Testing everything…
Hating
And
Avenging

Screaming at the horror clanging around
Inside their own
Skull.

Never wondering why

  They cheer so loudly

 When cruelty

  Tyranny

   And

     Hopelessness

   Are crushed

    By goodness

     Courage

      And

    Selfless, sacrificial love.

Never wondering where the tablet graven on their
hearts came from.

 Clutching at life.

  Reaching for stars.

 Hoping for something.

  Dreaming away horror.

 Living for love.

  Breathing for breathing.

  For the paradox of pleasure.

That it is to be

 Human.

I am No Denier of Science

- I was, at this point and unknowingly, a denier of science.

What do you see when you look at the moon,

The stars,

Your mother's eyes?

Where do you find hope?

A reason to live,

A reason to love?

When you say it is all nothing,

We are all just animals

No hope,

Just gain-less pain,

No reason

No season

For Peace and Love

And goodwill to men.

For we are just animals.

Just surviving.

Do what you want with your self,

Do what you want with your life,

It all ends eventually.

Ends with nothing.

No point to sacrifice

Or strife.

What of the future generation?

The higher evolved.

The inheritance of our pain.

You say the impossible happened.

So do I.

You say science and logic stepped aside.

I say He stepped in

And created both.

I am no denier of science,

I've looked the evidence through.

And I say, the ones following blindly,

Are those who tell half the truth.

You have thrown out your Humanity,

Tried to alter your own Reality,

You've tried to deny the responsibly

Of Morality,

Ignoring your own Mortality.

I am no denier of science,

I've looked the evidence through.

And I say ,

The only blind one

Is you.

I Will Be Waiting, Sinner

- Religious trauma (I was fucking 18).

Man, why do you shut your ears, try to ignore me,

the undeniable, creeping, certainty of death…

…the cries, the lies, your sins…

Coming for you…

Can you feel the creaking of your bones?

The pounding of your desperate, dying heart,

The blood screaming, tearing, pounding

Through your soft brain?

Go on, rush through life, ignore me.

I will be here. I will be waiting, sinner,

You will have your pay.

I will come for you.

I am coming for you.

Night

- I was obsessed (still am).

Half the world is falling asleep,

Half the world is coming to life.

Falling into the darkness of night

Full of senses, and of strife.

Night is a time for memory,

For ancient lullabies,

A time to lift your eyes to heaven,

To diamond trodden skies.

Night is a time for questions,

And newly ancient things.

Night gives terror feet,

And dreams, wings.

This is a time of opposites,

The darkness of the night,

Of ethereal beauty,

And cruel, gripping fright.

The Chrysalis

Like the stars a time of order,
Like the bat, of chaos too.
Night a time for truth,
In monochromatic hue.

The sky is velvet black,
The trees are darker still,
Whispering in airy voices,
To give mortal man a thrill.

Night is a time of peace,
A time for inner war,
Night, a time to sing songs
You've never heard before.

Night is a time for freedom,
Feet chained to the ground,
To sour in soul o'er every tree,
To sing with every sound.

Night is a time of contrast,
Of cold, terrifying mirth.
A time of whispers, and of life,
Of death, and of birth.

Night is a time for solitude,
Of healing from above,
A time for pain, and fear, and promises,
And never-ending love.

Half the world is going to sleep,
Half the world is coming alive,
Half the world immersed in darkness,
Living to survive.

Half the world cowers in fear,
And dare to shut their eyes.
But you and I, stare in wonder,
At diamond trodden skies.

Tonight

- Accidental B-track, panic in the same rhythm as my wonder.

Tonight is a night for doubt

For pain, and for tears

Tonight is a night for monsters,

Created by my own fears.

Tonight is a night for pondering

The demons at my heels.

Tonight is a night for silencing

The way my heart feels.

Tonight is a night for loneliness,

Protected by these walls.

No loving embrace

May penetrate these empty halls.

Tonight is a night to fight terrors,

But even when they're dead,

Scars trail on my soul

Teeth forever embed.

Tonight is a time of darkness

Through which no light may go

To think, and to cry, and to say

What others will never know.

Never Quiet

- I finally start writing fiction, and my escapist nature becomes in itself a fantasy.

Sometimes daily ordinary life seems pointless.

Nothing I am supposed to do is as demanding as my own imagination.

I distract myself, or rather my own brain stops me from doing the practical things. My mind is constantly crammed to the brim.

The spinning heavens, the glint of sunlight on trees and clouds, the faces of people I have never met, the images never leave.

Even worse are the stories. My math might be interesting, but it does not cry out, scream, for their story to be told, for them to escape the tight walls of my brain case. The looks, the gestures, the faces, the stories, the curdling battle cry, the pounding of hooves, the flow, the pulse of blood, the giving and taking of lives, and the crack and groan of the souls of trees, they never leave. They can be dampened, quieted, but never silenced.

Every day I must tell them, "not today" but they are still very distracting, and I tend to slip. The forming of a scene gazing out a window, the quick note, half-finished doodle, the pressure must be relieved, at least a little. Music is commanding enough to silence them, for a little while, until its very nature and intensity reminds me, and awakens them.

My mind is never quiet, it's enough to drive me mad.

- The College Years -

2016
(Reflection)

I'm still living at home but begin to creep away. I contemplate myself with less shame than before and leave rhyme as an afterthought.

Age: 19

The New Generation

-One year of college begins to open my eyes.

We are the new generation.

We're here

We're young

And we're terrified

Of past sedation

And future cyanide

We are the hopeless dreamers

We will stand

We will fall

And fall again

We are the new generation
Plagued by pessimism and hesitation
We're here
We think we'll fail
But we're here
Not ready to bail

We're here
We're young
And we're afraid
Of the futures
And the monsters
That we've made

We are the idle perfectionists
We will stand
We will fall
And fall again

We are the new generation

We are on our own
Surrounded

We will make music

Laced with chaos

Those songs which make you forget to breathe

We're here

We're young

Learning to love

Learning to sing

Hoping

    To dare

To hope

We will fall

And fall again

And rise

We are the new generation.

Instagram

-I wrote this at the drop of a hat for a boy who never gave two fucks about me (but I love lightning more than I ever thought I loved him).

Flashing fingers of sordid light

Reaching down to troubled water,

Shouting to all in sight.

Nature's child, Mayhem's daughter.

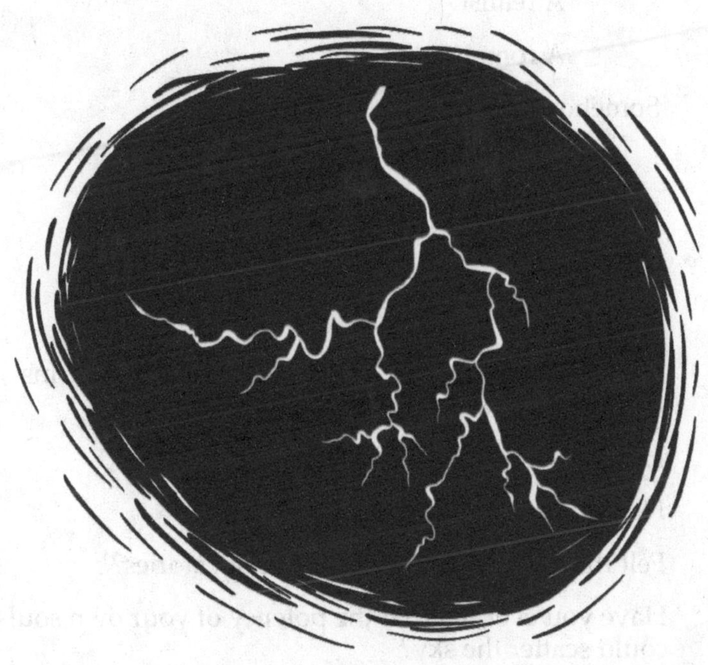

Me

-Writing about myself feels like an indulgence, a pride, but I will no longer apologize for it (or try not to).

I am a Pessimistic Optimist

I love equations and lightning

I am a night lover

      Always looking to sleep

I am

      A realist

      A romantic

Somehow both

The impossible, beautiful combination of artist

And scientist

Have you ever felt like you could spread your arms and ride the wind of music?

Have you ever felt the earth breathe?

Heard potent words in petrichor?

Felt the weight of a thousand untold stories?

Have you ever felt that the potency of your own soul could scatter the sky?

Have you felt upwelling tears at the mere flutter of a
bird?

A single word?

      A weighty, familiar story?

         A small surprise?

            That pair of eyes?

               A tiny hidden glory?

I am a thinker.

I think

I stare out of a window

See everything

See nothing

Hear something like a hum

Thoughts, feelings, hurts

      Colors, ideas, images

Words

      Songs

Stories

Buzz around my head like negative charges in an
electron cloud.

I am, confidently hesitant

    What is this pseudo-bravery?

I pretend to be strong

I grew older

Thought I broke out of my shell

I became foolish

Easily rebuked to silence in realization of my folly

    No one cares if it is my shell or my skin

        They may crush me

    This is pseudo-strength

I am trusting

    I trust faith

    Advice

    Opinion

But

    Dreams

    Feelings

    Tears

        Fears

These are made of glass

These are not made for careless hands

With these I trust

    Very few

        Very little

I am, forgetful

Forget

       My phone

       My keys

       Myself

Forget that no one else is me

       That I am a stranger

Forget that no one cares

       That the sky was blue today

       That my snake smiled at me

       That I sat under the stars

       And sang

I forget that no one cares

       Their eyes are small

They

       Are nothing like me

I forget that I am a stranger.

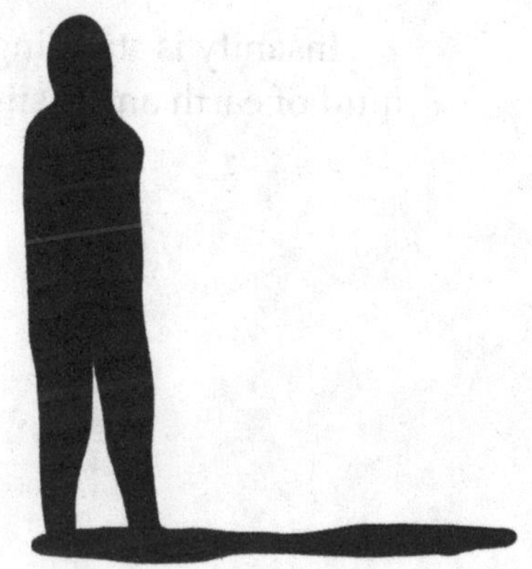

Insanity

-I saw myself as insane. (In some ways I still do.)

The world has a very narrow definition of insanity. A word coupled with images of comedic levels of blood and maniacal laughter. I would not go so far as to say that everyone is insane, there are some that are clearly not, and yet, we did not see them as children.

Insanity is smiling at a stranger with no inkling of what kind of person they could be.

Insanity is opening your arms to the morning dew, as if it could return the embrace.

Insanity is smiling through tears, it is kneeling before nothing, it is standing in the center of a storm and laughing.

Insanity is standing with feet planted in the black mud of earth and tasting heaven.

Church Notes

-I drew so many demons and monsters in the house of god, along with the angels who slew them. (There was violence in this dogma, and felt I the pain of the monster even as I prayed to the spear.)

Some Know What Others Do Not

-I contemplate paradox and think myself wise.

Some know what others do not.

      That tragedies are often comic,

And that comedy is often the face of real tragedy.

Some know what others do not.

That only pessimists know real optimism

That the wish for sleep is not the same as the wish for
tomorrow

And that leaving home is sometimes a vain pursuit of
the same home.

Some know what others do not.

That the line between logical thinking and imagination

is as sure as the boundary between the clouds and the
sky.

That the eyes are not the window to the soul,

but a periscope to the heart.

That the faster you go, the slower you think.

And that to treasure memories is to wish to make
more.

Some know what others do not.

That only fools call themselves wise and the wise are
very few

That it has never been decided if night and day are

at war

or

in love.

That love is action and real hate is fear.

That fear is either born of

ignorance

or

understanding.

That knowledge is not absolute,

But...

Some know what others do not.

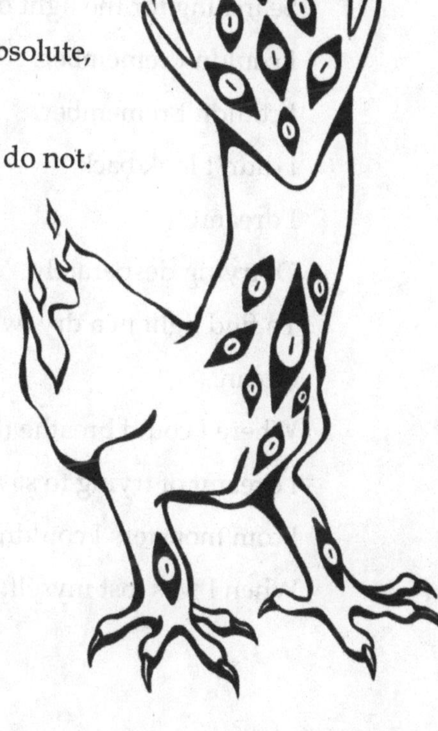

Strange Dream

-I try not to find interpretations in my dreams, but I do appreciate the poetry.

I dreamt, I was in a world

Of plastic

And the color pink.

Where the game was easy.

Where I was re-shown how to throw

Every time I forgot.

It wasn't right.

I left,

Though I was warned I could not return.

I went into the blackness,

Searching for the light of a love

I couldn't remember.

I couldn't remember.

I didn't look back.

I dreamt,

Of trying desperately

To find light in a dry, windy

Ocean,

Where I could breathe the dust.

I dreamt of trying to save lost children

From monsters I couldn't see,

When I was lost myself.

I dreamt,

Of someone stronger than me

Swinging on clustered chains.

And as they went,

The chains changed to vines,

And then to the ropes we played on in sunny days.

And then it ended.

And we fell to the forest floor,

Forgetting the quest for light.

My Colors

-I try to find boxes to fit myself in besides "sinner" and "failure".

If people were made of colors,

I am fairly certain what I would be.

If someone could peer into my essence and found what made my soul,

I'm certain what they would find is

Grey and gold.

Grey,

Grey for my eyes

Grey for the uncertain glances of my careful, noticing eyes

Grey for the way I feel as though I put my emotions on my sleeves, and find misinterpretation in the face of another

Grey for the watery confidence with which I engage those I wish would like me

Grey for the way I am nothing special in their eyes

Grey for fear

Grey for hesitance

Grey for loneliness

Grey for my ability to sink into someone else's memory as an unwelcome stain

Grey for clouds and tears and songs

Grey for deep breaths and lingering moments

But not only grey...

But a warm, rosy gold of the nature you find in
sunlight.

Gold,

      Gold for my hair,

Gold for the shimmering, constant warmth like my hair
in the sun

Gold for genuine smiles

Gold for my ability to find joy in the smallest things

Gold for beautiful knowledge

Gold for the dazzling excitement of new days and
changing seasons

Gold for the comforting constancy of home

Gold for loyalty

For the feeling of creating something new
Gold for love

Grey and gold

This is me

Grey and gold

In love with

Green and blue.

Feelings

-I begin identifying as "writer", and though I cringe at my early fiction, I do not have the heart to call the label wrong. This is a young person's description of love and it is clichéd but it was not born of infatuation and, once again, I cannot call it wrong.

Some feelings cannot be described, they can only be felt. You cannot begin to try to place them into the brain of another soul with the power of ink and paper.

Some feelings can only be felt.

So what is left for the writers?

Those people who feel the need to scrawl impossible dreams onto papers and computer screens?

What of us?

We can only try.

Excitement is perhaps the easiest to describe. A building, lumpy sort of feeling that tingles through your fingers and always manages to make its way onto your face.

Doubt feels itchy and fuzzy, it clings to the inside of your skin like an unwanted tattoo.

Happiness is velvety and exciting, swirling around your face and illuminating your eyes, however short its duration.

Anxiety is like static and tangled strings, wrapping around your heart and your stomach, curling into your forehead and making it hard to breath.

Fear is one of the worst. It is anxiety's older brother, and it is ice cold. It is gripping and freezing and squeezes your heart.

There are some emotions without names.

That mix of contentment and exhaustion that feels like the weight of a blanket, slowing the world and allowing the mind to just be.

That deep, sorrowful pleasure which accompanies the purposeful touch of another.

And the feeling of opening your arms to a small, beautiful corner of the world, and somehow seeing everything.

Yes, perhaps it is impossible to describe emotion; but there is one thing which is most certainly impossible to describe.

Love.

Love is not an emotion, and yet it the culmination and anticipation of every emotion. It is choice. It is action. Yet, undoubtedly something that can be felt; and something which people have been trying to describe since man was created.

Love is impossible to describe.

Mostly because it is nearly impossible even to feel it as a whole.

Grief is impossible to describe.

Grief is impossible to describe because grief is born of love.

And just as words are wholly inadequate for emotion, so are they inadequate for grief.

For grief is not an emotion. It is the culmination and anticipation of every emotion. It is not a choice. But a consequence of choice. A consequence of love.

It feels like breaking.

Like living as a part of something which once was whole, or should have been.

It is the most terrifying sort of pain.

For it is not only felt in the body.

Yet we still love.

For love is more powerful than grief. It is the most powerful thing in the universe. No matter how much it hurts, or how deeply it breaks us. Because love is not an emotion.

Love is a word inadequate to describe the impossible culmination of everything we are.

Permission

-We'll see if she was right.

I wonder if anyone will read what I have written,
I wonder if they will have permission if they do.
None of this is really worth perfecting, publishing, or
transforming into real poetry.

Not that it makes it any less enjoyable. For now, I
will write for the simple joy of cursive with a ballpoint
pen and the slight relief of placing another thought into
tangible form.

I have so many.

Some will never be realized, many never should be.

Perhaps a slim few will be read, perhaps with
permission even.

I am not sure anyone would care for the ramblings
of a confused soul; but my cursive does look nice on
this paper.

What is Poetry?

-I still ask this question (confused by free verse).

What is Poetry?

How do we define

something that is undefined as

part of its definition?

Because I place these words like this

Is this free verse poetry?

It's more of an inquiry.

Certainly the rhythm of words

Makes poetry,

But

There is something else.

Something undefined which

Brushed the corners

of the author's soul.

Something that speaks in

The white space.

The words left unsaid,
Concepts left unexplained,
Some small important part of the poet that is left to be
Misunderstood.

Something that reaches out to others
And estranges them.

And we call it
Poetry.

Many faces

*-I reckon with my sudden ability to make my daydreams real,
and flirt with rhyme again.*

There are many faces

in my head

Many living

    All dead

Every time I'm left alone

    They crawl out

From inside my bones

They are part of me

    This makes sense

I created them

    From what

Makes no difference

They are lovers

    Dreamers, killers

And I cannot see

    Whether or not, they are made

From me

They are part of the stories
I create every night
They live and they die
Struggle and fight.

They do not know me
I know them quite well
Yet they silently plead for me
Their stories to tell

I move out. I throw myself into making the dreams of fantasy into something substantial (the glory of making something new with someone I love). Yet I forget to write anything but fiction.

(I free myself of what I thought was home).

Age: 20

A Story Begins

- I thought of writing as something more fantastical than I might now, but there was always a realist and a dramatist warring in my head.

There is only one way that a story really begins. Whether it alights upon the innermost feelings on a dreary day, hits like a train in the midst of a particularly passionate song, or scatters itself inside of dreams, a story must plant itself inside the mind of a writer.

This person may or may not know they are a writer yet, all they know is that they have words and pictures flowing through their heads at an alarming rate, and the only way to ease the pressure, is to write.

Tiny Lightning Storm

- A little thing with a very literal meaning, the second poem about lightning I wrote for Instagram, but for me this time.

When sky is dark,

And mind is loud,

Paint tiny stars

Above a cloud.

When fingers buzz

With unknown emotion,

Paint a tiny

Blackened ocean.

When head is cold,

And blood is warm,

Paint a tiny

Lightning storm.

2018
(Exposure)

Shame and Fury and Awakening. I battle the loneliness in myself and the wrongness of the world.

Age: 21

Devotional (for Women)

-Written backwards. The fourth and final entry in a coloring book devotional — the last time I ever tried.

1 Peter 1:2
"Grace and peace be yours in abundance."

Grace always, grace flowing like springs from Heaven.

But peace is harder to find.

I feel like I was made without that capacity, the truth of my flawed soul (its own demon) tearing at it.

I am left with apathy, the bleeding corpse of peace.

Lord, you said it was peace without understanding, and I believe it.

Apology

*- White shame and the fury of learning how deep the wrongs
go. (Why must we wait until college to know the truth?)*

Can I just offer an Apology?

We're not the marble statues we claimed to be.

We're nothing but the sons of sons, who threw you in
the sea.

We're just as soft, just as fleshy

    Just as easy to break

As every other man who ever dared to

    Take

and take and take.

There are no scars on my back,

No chains on my wrists,

Only those common tortures,

Of trying to exist.

Can I offer an Apology?

We're just the same,

    Just as greedy, just as needy.

Forgive us,

> For pretending we were holy.

> For pretending we knew

The colors of the angels.

Forgive us for hiding behind manufactured smiles.
Forgive us for being afraid.

> But hundreds of years worth of manipulation,

> It doesn't just go away.

Can I offer an apology?

For existing in this skin of mine?

> For the color of every sin of my father's fathers?

We're really just fragile
Sick fools.

> Just like everyone.

Can I offer an apology?

For the bleached atmosphere of our literacy?

> For the thin scrapings of what we call, "all of
history?"

> For the screens so white it burns my eyes?

Can I offer an apology?

For every wrong that wasn't mine.

For every sin I benefit from.

For the white dust of the bones that built this nation.

Our remains all smell the same.

Can I offer an apology?

For my own helplessness.

For my own unwillingness to be anything else.

For the way I cheer for the fight from the sidelines.

Can I offer an apology?

For my people.

My country.

For the blue veins you can see through my skin.

For my desperate need of a sun who scorns me.

We were never white.

(Except in death)

We were never the marble statues we claimed to be.

I Am But a Door Standing Open

- Always lonely, always longing, there's a few that make it inside and I'm grateful.

I am but a door standing open.

Not the open door of a shop in sunshine,

    With the beckoning of the open sign and sweet smells.

Not the open door of a public house,

    With swaying shadows and booming music swells.

Not the open door of a townhouse,

    Flung open by loving hands pushing away snow.

Not the open door of a mansion,

    Held with careful gloves in wishful glow.

I am a door standing open

    (Not all the way open)

No decorations without,

    Only darkness within.

I am the door left standing open.

    Threatening.

I am the door to your grandparents' basement,

    With darkness creeping up the wooden stairs.

I am the door to the unused store room,

    Where forbidding sign in clear text declares.

I am the door you see but do not answer,

    Your feet quickening upon intended trek.

I am the door you wonder about but never enter,

    Daring your friends and craning your neck.

I am the door left standing open.

    Welcoming.

I am the door with hidden joys and secrets

    (The monsters here have been waiting for you).

I am the door with lonely corners and treasures,

    Only for them who dare to walk through.

I am the door hiding cozy libraries,

    Past the rubble and down the winding stairs.

I am the door hiding a hearth of a soul,

    Past the webs and the bones and the cares.

I am a door standing open

    (Not all the way open)

No decorations without,

    Only a guess what's within.

I am but the sum of everything beyond myself.

I am but a door standing open.

Real Estate

- Fury yet again. It feels like it isn't just my own.

I heard they tore down the cabin that used to be my home, that they cut down the tree I thought was the most beautiful in the world

(the one that stood alone with arms uplifted like the statue of an old goddess)

that they tore up the garden in the center of the drive that had grown for a decade into its own sort of monster

(I had thought those lilies could have taken over the world)

and I cried.

I cried, with shuddering shoulders and an acidic heart, for the wild, beautiful things who can no longer cry for themselves, for the timber stripped of everything but lonely, dying trees, and for the prairies turned to manicured lawns.

I cried because the man who did it found no fault in it, because those things had no use to him that he could see.

I cried for all those who do not try to understand, for all those who find no beauty and no order in wild things, for all those who believe supremacy means something to God.

Foolish, short-sighted, narrow-minded man. Did you think you were above reproach?

Utility, only Utility. The masses cry for Utility, opening hungry mouths and greedy hands.

(For nothing without a clear use deserves to exist.)

So we shun artists and dreamers and the weak, knowing in our grand human wisdom that they could do us no good.

We shun the green things, forgetting that everything is connected.

(We do not shoot ourselves in the foot but in the face)

Forgetting that every action has its equal, that Nature is a system of which we are a part

(that retribution is built into the cycle of life).

Forgetting the God who gave us the power to kill is one of temperance and kindness.

We kill ourselves with necessity, create our own endless deserts, and shackle our fate with concrete.

I cried, not only for the beautiful, imperfect place that had been my home, but for the disrespect.

The Hubris.

What is there for those of us who understand? Those of us with tree souls and bird hearts, who pick up crows' feathers and stare at the clouds? Those of us who rage against an extinction for we which we are partly to blame? What of us?

There is only to embrace what beauty remains, and to mourn the approaching grey.

(We weave rope only to hang ourselves with it)

(And the tree does not oppose the weight)

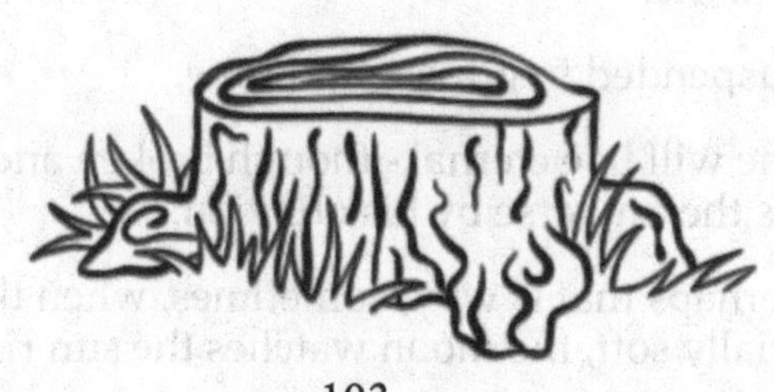

The Moon Watched the Sun Rise

- A love poem.

I saw the sun rise this morning. All the edges of the world had turned to rainbows, the night long banished.

Still, the moon stayed.

I think she stayed to watch the sun rise too. Hanging high in the west in silent, pastel luxury, forgetting her own duties if only for a moment.

She was as pure a white as I have ever seen her, untouched by the golden horizon.

Perhaps the sun watched her too, sad that he had never seen her in her proper place, the crown jewel in the abyss of his absence.

I think he knows her light is truly his.

All the better for him to see her face. He doesn't mind sharing, he has plenty.

She accepts his gift, but she knows.

I think she knows.

That in time past time she will watch him die.

That the world she knows will be swallowed into his used-up heart, into the absence of him.

And she,

She,

A stone,

Suspended in gravity and time,

She will live eternal - though broken and scattered across the universe by his oblivion.

Perhaps that is why, sometimes, when the sky is especially soft, the moon watches the sun rise.

Perhaps he laughs at her solemnity, continuing to give and to burn.

Giving and giving and burning and burning into his piece of the galaxy.

Does he know?

The moon knows.

Perhaps that is why lonely, knowing souls find solace in her face, in the cold reflected light of Sun's giving.

Even the ocean reaches for her.

Whispering

Teach us,

Wandering one

Watching one

Lonely one

Knowing one.

Teach us to love what is not eternal.

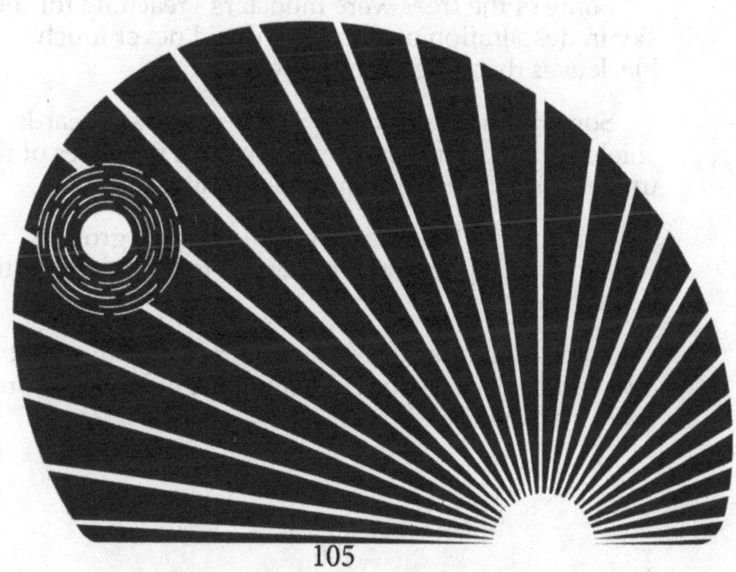

My Forest

- My compassion towards unwanted things allows me to have some grace for myself (I may not stand up for myself as much as I should, but my monsters never did deserve that kind of treatment). I'm learning.

In a daydream

Or a nightmare,

I don't remember,

They are the same,

I fell into my own forest.

It was stranger and more familiar than any place I had ever been, and I did not know if it was my soul or the place where my soul lives.

Some of the trees were trees - living and dead, woody and wet, no senses to tell them they existed.

Some of the trees were monsters - reaching for the sky in desperation of stars they could never touch, black eyes dripping with sap tears.

Some of the trees were wise men - mossy beards shielding long ears that have heard the promises of the universe and tried to comprehend them.

Some of the trees had legs - tearing the ground where they stepped with no regard to anything but the need to be away.

Some of the trees were hollow, but not empty - their own vibrancy drained and a hundred holes and worm trails marring their bones.

Some of my monsters lived in those hollow trees.

I will not tell you how I knew it, but they were mine, as much as the forest was mine. Whether they have always been me I do not know.

Some of them are snakes, stunning, black, shimmering like starlight under the moon. They move like grace and perfection, deadly and afraid. I love them.

I cry when I look at them.

Because they hide.

Because they are beautiful.

Because the beasts of the light would trample them underfoot and call it god's work.

Some of my monsters are wolves.

Not many of them.

They are made of flames, of molten metal, of the cores of stars. They roam in packs about my forest, burning trees to ashy shells.

My wolves are silent.

Almost.

They become restless, waking ancient instincts to howl, to scream, to burn, and sometimes I let them. When the space is clear and the damage manageable, I let them cleanse and screech.

Some of my monsters are rivers.

They swell and pulse up and down hills as they please, drowning. They water my trees, but they have no master.

I build levies, but my rivers are not rivers.

They are old gods.

My wolves run beside them in a frenzy of panic and joy.

Some of my monsters are birds.

Hooked beaks and talons curved for gutting warm bellies. They are bitter and sharp, eyes snapping towards every movement, sensing threats, assessing their own hatred for the others.

Their wings are made from knives, but I let them perch on my shoulders until my skin is ribbons, until I become the redness they feast on.

They are ancient things.

Some of my monsters have no shape.

They are made from the colors under my skin.

They have claws and coils, teeth and water, they are blind, but they know this forest well.

They know the shape of the keys on the gates and levies, they know where to find the little cabin at the center of it all. They find pleasure in stroking claws over the pulsing thing that is protected there.

Listen to the crunch and rustle of leaves, the rage and the dripping of the water, listen to the cries and songs of my monsters. There is a beat, a music only some can hear.

I hope others can hear it, only I have walked in the deepest parts of this forest.

My monsters do not bite so hard.

They are beautiful if you know their names.

If you know the snakes hold the forest together with their coils.

If you know the wolves hunt for something that only they can find.

If you know the rivers only search for a belonging place.

If you know the birds are the guardians of the skies and that they have fought greater dragons.

Monsters

- I was never afraid of anything but mankind and emptiness.

They make monsters

Out of animal amalgamations

They prey on our base instincts to flee at the sight of bloody, dripping teeth

They prey on our knowledge that that many eyes are too many, those sort of claws are too long

They prey on our disgust, on our knowledge that that smell is not of the living

But there are those of us who know that the greatest monster is made of empty space and silence.

Consuming nothingness.

Iowa Gothic

- I love what this place was - what it could be. (I fear it too)

Neither the endless skies of the West, nor the endless cities of the East. Here in the middle, in the middle we understand.

We understand. Some more than others, and most with no voice to describe it.

Here in the beating bosom of this continent.

Here the trees are blacker than the sky, reaching at once for the stars and for the slumbering malice beneath the bedrock. You never hear them scream, whether felled by storm, or ax, or time. They know it is their time. Devoured by fungus, by fire, by man, they understand.

You don't come to Iowa; you end up here.

Some leave. They claim it is too boring, too flat. Perhaps they are right, perhaps they are only afraid of the rhythm of their own lives, afraid of the silence, seeking for distractions. They do not wish to hear what the moths have to say.

Some of us are born here, born with black dirt in our veins. And we grow. We grow like the corn, and you can hear it. Faces lifted and feet planted, we bend but we rarely break.

Storms are born here, swirling up from nothing but the anger in the dirt, and you know you should run and cover your head, but you can do nothing but stare. Dark thunderheads grow taller, decapitated by the winds of heaven. The thunder cracks and rolls like the warm pavement under your feet. You feel it in your sternum, and you can't run, you can't hide, because you finally understand the word hallelujah.

You have black dirt in you veins and the lightning makes the grass grow.

Here we understand, even the children could tell you. Here there is a smaller distance between man and the world. There is a terror in the spaces between the blades of grass, holy absolution in the heavy air. There are voices that whisper: from the high canopies, in the long shadows, warm behind your ear. "You belong here."

You sit with a sleepy disaster in your chest and tears slip down your cheeks. You understand. You are home.

Here the world watches you, a billion eyes and only some you can see, stare from the cracks and shadows of the world. The yellow moon between the branches is another. We do not mind. Here we understand. We watch back.

Here the roads are fragile, living things, hungry as an infant apocalypse. We fill the cracks with gold and blood, but they are never healed, never satisfied. They break and are reborn, resisting any form but black and straight and forever. Here the ground breaths heavily and asphalt cracks.

Here in the beating bosom of this continent.

There are few who remember what it looked like before, few who forget. The dirt remembers. It yields the food of the world with persuasion, but it has never been tamed. One summer's neglect brings a vengeful remembering, and foxes creep through forests of wildflowers.

Nothing is empty here.

Here we understand.

Life comes from life and is fed by death.

Animals give birth and bean sprouts break the surface of the ground, heads held high. It is not as different as you might think.

Here, home is a feeling, it is a belonging, it is an understanding.

We understand.

We belong here.

There is no force under heaven we have not felt.

There are no fences without gates.

We will always return here, our bones will feed the milkweed and the chaos, and our blood will turn to red clay, deer prints in the riverbank.

This is the doorway to everywhere.

No one's destination.

You don't come to Iowa. You end up here.

2019
(Revelation)

Age: 22

What happened to that little girl who wrote rhymes about spiders?

Dead Hope

- Impermanence and exhaustion (my whole generation are old souls).

We were made searching creatures. Uncontented by any present. Cursed to wish for what we do not have, to neglect what we do, until it is stripped from us forever.

There is nowhere that is our home forever, there is no person, no joy, that lasts forever.

The weight of even these short years threaten to crush the hope that I was born with. I can feel it, running out of me like blood, and it is the world that has wounded me - not fatally, not dramatically, but little by little, slice by slice - until my head swims, and I am knee deep in my own life-blood, surrounded by the rotting smell of dead hope.

It looks grim, but I continue.

I dread the years as a prisoner his sentence, yet the looming of death is no less comforting than the pain of living.

I believe it is the human condition. Find me in the dark corners where I cannot see the blood. Find me with the green things, where my body will nourish the trees. I am tired of this human condition.

Girl Who Cried Wolf

- Imposter syndrome had me then as now.

Mesmerizing,

The way a corpse on the highway draws your eye.

A quiet honor like the promise of a dry river bed.

And I feel like if I cry for help,

I'll be the girl who cried wolf,

The drowning victim who doesn't realize
they're standing in the
shallow end.

      Because couldn't
it be so much worse than
this?

    It'll get better....

        It has to.

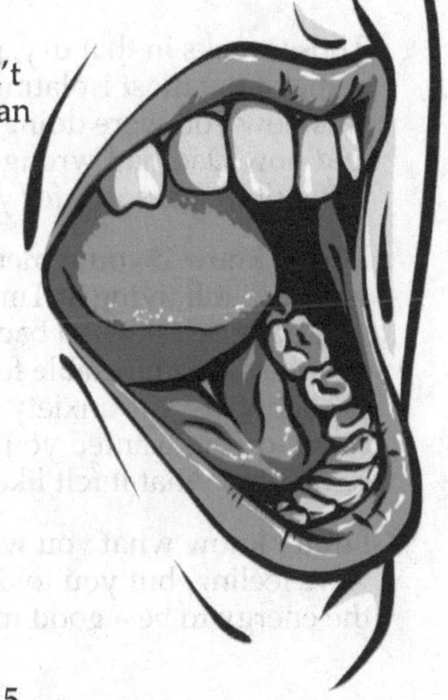

Dear Mom

-Snippets of an eleven-page letter I wrote to my mother that I knew I would never send. It was full of lies I told myself, melting through the paper like acidic ink, but these parts... these parts I started to believe.

I didn't know how to respond when you said you felt like you had done something wrong, and you asked if there was something you needed to apologize for. You acted like you wanted to know, that you wanted to know us better – me better – but I didn't believe you...

You've taught me things I'm proud to know, but Mom, I don't know how to tell you that you taught me how to be afraid.

My body doesn't remember how it felt to hug you and feel safe....

I have tried to forgive you for Arizona, but it's hard when I doubt you know what a hell those months were for me. You took us from every person and comfort but you, and all I thought about, all day, was going away – back home...

...it felt very much like you wanted us to suffer.

Those weeks in that dry, god-forsaken wasteland were some of the most isolating in my life. And all I heard was how you were doing, and how you were suffering, and how Dad had wronged you. And it became very difficult to feel sorry for you. It still is...

I don't know if you remember, but there was a night we were still living at Timberedge when I came to you because I'd had a bad dream. There were a lot of strange, uncomfortable feelings in my head, and it was probably just the anxiety of growing up...but I actually came to you, wanted you to comfort me, and I don't remember what it felt like to be that brave.

I don't know what you were dealing with, what you were feeling, but you told me that you, "didn't have the energy to be a good mommy tonight."

I try to forgive you for that too…but I needed you, and you couldn't be there for me, and I went back to bed to deal with those feelings myself, and never went to you again when there were monsters in my head. I still think it was probably the safest option for me, and the least of a burden on you. Still, I can't help think of that night every time you say I keep my feelings to myself.

The most bitter parts of me want to laugh in your face. To scream, "You made me this way!" And how am I supposed to come to you with my monsters when they're shaped like your anger and your expectations and your threats?

The bitter parts of me also tend to laugh when you say you're a 'sensitive person' – that you can tell when someone is hurting. If that's true then it means you saw my suffering and did nothing, and I hope that it isn't true. I think you are very perceptive of every wrong but your own...

I don't believe you've ever really wanted to know my opinion or what I was feeling, because you don't ever believe there could be a situation were I was right and you were wrong.

And there's that bitter part of me again, laughing about all the times you've accused me of needing to be right...

I know it's selfish, and wrong, but there's a part of me that wants so badly for you to know how you made me suffer, to see the irreversible damage and to be sorry, actually sorry. As much as you've forced your perspective on me, I wonder if you've ever really tried to consider mine.

Then again, you don't know me. You don't know what's important to me, you don't know my doubts or my wonderings any more than you know my desires. So, I guess I'll start there. I wish it weren't this way, but one of my greatest desires in the world is to feel safe, and right now I can't feel that around you. You've always been a force of danger and uncertainty in my life.

Maybe that can change, but I don't know.

Nothing Special
- Imposter syndrome pt. 2.

I'm nothing special.

I'm sure this suffering is merely human.

There is nothing so special about loneliness.

It is natural for us to feel that our soul floats freely in the dark.

No reason for me to make it a big deal.

Two things are human.

To feel loneliness.

And to wish it were not so.

The Noise

*- I think I had a panic attack listening to my parents watch
America's Got Talent compilations in the room next to mine...I
don't watch much tv anymore.*

I feel as though I've seen behind the veil

You're trying to make me feel something

Trying to make me cry

Trying to make me weep for the cardboard cutouts of
misery and inspiration that you shove into my face

But I already know the world is misery

I don't need yours

I don't need you to tell me what's terrible

I don't need you to tell me what's beautiful or great

I don't need to be told what is honorable

I get sick of people

People are my enemy

      And I'm the worst of them

They take

They take they take they take

They carve out their eyes for the joy of the sins they
commit

I hate your lovely voices

Give me something ugly

Something real

Let me put my hands in the dirt and cover my hideous
human form

Let me become the dirt and the sky and the air

Give me something like the taste of blood in my
mouth, the terrible, drying viscosity

That's real

That's real

How *cute*

How *talented*

How *incredible*

Please

Please just shut up
Put away your plastic eyes and chrome teeth
Dive with me into the woods and let the mosquitoes
suck you dry

Feel the splinters in your fingers and the leeches on
your ankles

Feel the true spirit of nature

Eat

Be eaten

Be real

I'm so tired of pretending

I'm so tired of glorifying nothing

There is so little left worth glorifying

There is so little left worth glorifying

TELL THE TRUTH

TELL THE TRUTH

FOR THE SAKE OF ALL HUMANITY PLEASE CAN'T WE JUST START TELLING THE TRUTH

I'm so tired of pretending

There's no bite left to these cobras

These nazis are pretending to be teddy bears

And I've never liked teddy bears

Bears are not cuddly

They will tear through your skull with their claws and return to their honey because they tell the truth

Because they know the truth

Eat

And be eaten

I'm so tired of existing

So terrified to die

Why does this cheering create such disgust in my throat

There's something like bile in my unsaid words

I can't breath

I just might scream if I do

What an inspiration

What a sad story

Look at them, they're living

STOP

STOP MAKING INSPIRATIONAL STORIES FROM TRAGEDIES

LOOK THEY CAN DO IT

THEY CAN OVERCOME MOUNTAINS

STOP

JUST STOP

AND BOWL OVER THE MOUNTAINS!

I'm sorry...

Was I shouting

No?

Good

No one will care what I'm saying anyway

No one hears the screaming of the world

They filter out everything but the cheers

And gold is nothing but plastic

And diamond is nothing but chains

And

My cynicism feels like enlightenment sometimes

But I know that it's slowly killing me

Can you feel the hands tightening around my fragile throat

They are mine
They are the world's

They are existing

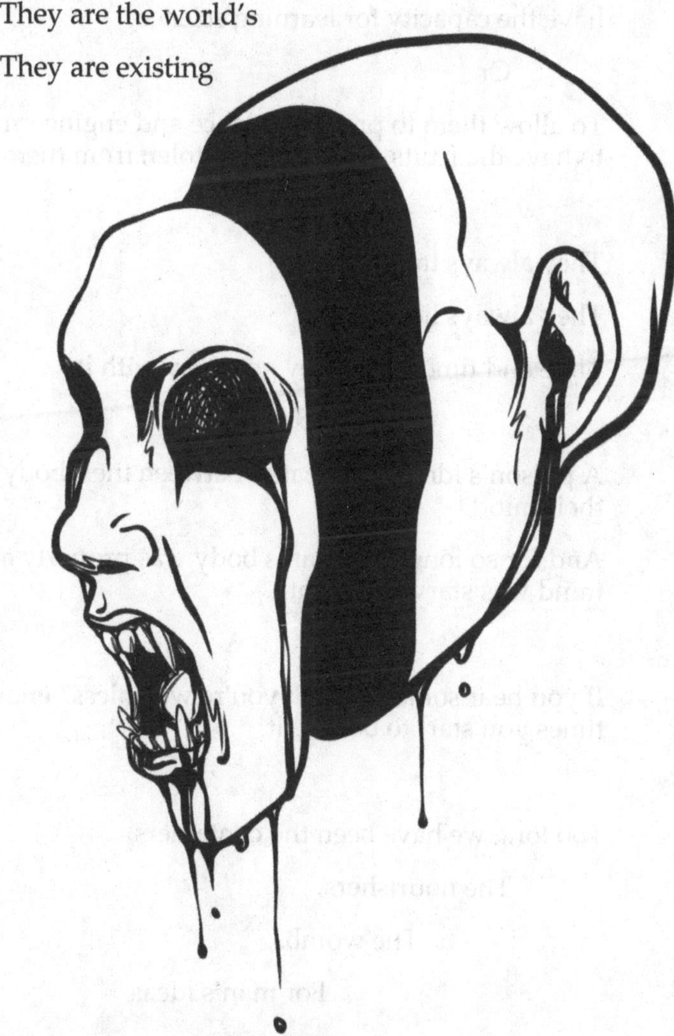

Take me away from the noise

Uncredited

- The ramblings my school project didn't see.

I don't know which is more cruel

To deny that an entire half of human beings do not have the capacity for learning science

      Or

To allow them to practice science and engineering only to have the fruits of their labor stolen from them.

They always take,

They always lie

Time and time again they get away with it.

A person's identity is seated between their body and their mind.

And for so long a woman's body was property and her mind was starved to death.

If you hear someone say "you're worthless" enough times you start to believe it.

Too long we have been the containers,

      The nourishers,

          The wombs,

              For man's ideas.

I do not wish to take glory from those who deserve it,

But a man who still requires breastmilk is not a man at all.

Let the vampires die in the light.

Words

- Typing and overthinking.

It's so strange,

That when I try to focus on which letters I'm typing

Suddenly I don't know where they are.

I have to look down at my hands.

I am lost,

Abruptly,

In my own room,

My own realm.

Everything that was familiarity and rhythm suddenly lost,

A blank space in my rapid consciousness.

But when I don't think,

When I don't care,

It is easy.

These are my fingers.

This is my keyboard.

And I know these letters like the back of my hand,

Or the smile of old friends.

It is then that I have no thought at all but the words that I want to create.

I think too much.

I know this.

I stare at these little black shapes on a white screen and wonder how I can glean so much meaning from them.

What witchcraft is literacy.

These words are forever,

Though they mean everything or nothing,

Lost in binary code.

You Have Never Seen the Sun

- A rack of plants in one of my classrooms sparks in me some poorly hidden sorrow.

To that row of plants on the bottom level of a growing rack in the corner of a cinderblock room:

What must it be like, to be a plant and to have never seen the sun?

We have what we need here, the nutrition and the water.

But you have never seen the sun.

We are not subject to the whims of other lives, our roots unbothered by digging creatures, and our leaves untrimmed by herbivores.

But you have never seen the sun.

We are never crowded or overshadowed by the limbs of trees or choked by weeds.

But you have never seen the sun.

We are never frozen by winter, or scorched by summer, we have everything we need.

But you have never seen the sun.

How can we miss something we have never known?

I have no answer. But all I can think of is the brush of sunlight against my cheek after the clouds part. All I can think is what a greater joy it must be to be a plant, and grow and thrive from that energy, and I do not think I could be content under the harsh blue UV radiation of that indoor grow light.

But I am not sure.

The sun can kill too.

- The Now -

2020 (Panoramic)

A year we will not soon forget, broken-off plans, twisting dreams, locked-in panic, and new revelations.

Age: 23

[Before Pandemic]

AU

- A love poem for no one.

I can't help feeling like I'm mourning something that never was, someone I never knew.

And I think about those alternate universes people create for their favorite fictional characters.

The one where they meet as children and grow up together.

The one where they live in a different place, a different time.

The one where they meet as adults, colliding into each other's lives with a vortex of destiny.

The one where they live in space,

Or in a little town.

The one where they meet in a coffee shop.

And I feel like I live in the universe where I never meet you. You're someone else, somewhere else, that I can't get to, but it's these moments of mourning I can't help but believe in soulmates

Because something is missing. I know it is.

I feel like I live in the universe where you died young and I drift through reality knowing that it's wrong,

That the author never meant it to be this way.

It feels silly to say it out loud.

But I miss you.

Why does it seem like I'm half of the concept of forever?

Why was I born with such loyalty in my bones if I was never going to meet someone who understands the choice in destiny.

I'm happy.

Or I think I am.

But the silence and the emptiness is greater than any monster on earth.

Some part of me thinks (knows?) it will be this way forever, and I can't tell if it's the scared little girl under my skin (she's often wrong) or my ancient soul (she rarely is).

I'm Not Sick

February 2020

-I've wondered a long time if there was something wrong with me, but there isn't a doctor to tell me if I'm just torturing myself or if I'm truly broken - they can't see past the fact I can still do my job - that I can still look them in the eye...I blame capitalism.

I'm not sick

But my hands are shaking

My bones feel like they wish they could escape my flesh

I'm not sick

But my stomach is turning

And the taste and texture of what I should love makes me wretch

I'm not sick

But there's sweat on my skin

And the claws clenching my heart are not mine

I'm not sick

There's no virus inside me

No temperature, no symptoms beside

I'm not sick

There's just this panic that will not leave me

Just the fuzz inside my mind

I'm not sick

But I am hurting

With no proper excuse

I'm not sick

But I'm not functioning

This is not something I
choose

I'm not sick

I'm just crying

The ever-looming
panic waiting to
take me

I'm not sick

I won't take leave

There's nothing you
can catch from me

Dream: February 27

-I dream in color, and the goddess was so blue

I dreamed of wolves and gods,

And a misplaced warrior

Who only ever wanted to belong,

- To stand on the prow of a dry ship and revel in the magnitude and chaos of the world -

Who watched great powers embrace others,

(The god of the sea had a fish's body and a woman's face)

Rejoicing with the chosen

Yet with that small voice inside him wondering,

Who will choose me?

Only to be told by that great deep voice

"You will replace me,

the god of destruction and woe.

And I am afraid."

I dreamed of a cursed man,

That lonely misplaced warrior,

Walking along the paths of the world knowing he could not die,

And oh, he was sad

He was so sad I felt in in my breastbone.

"You will replace me,"

Says the god of destruction.

"I am afraid,"

Says the god of fear,

"And I cannot change what is to come."
They wait in agonizing wandering -
The misplaced warrior and the god of destruction -
Neither desiring their fate,
Living in doomed invincibility.

**[Lock-in back at my parents' - a mental health mistake,
I'm never going back.]**

Fury

March 2020

*- There is nothing that could make a man understand the rage
that is in us.*

Perhaps those ancient Greek men knew more than they
let themselves understand when they called the Furies
by women's names and gave them women's bodies.

Perhaps they saw it…

Divine Retribution

In the eyes of their frightened daughters and their
hurting wives.

Perhaps they saw that secret violence of righteous
anger in their silence.

It was all they could do to call the furies female,

For whenever was a man's anger divine…

It seems all they could do was to pray for mercy to the
hurting voices they had created, and to imagine it was
other men the voices were screaming at.

In the end, we are not goddesses…

We are only left with our Fury.

[Somehow, they could see our god-hood but not our
humanity]

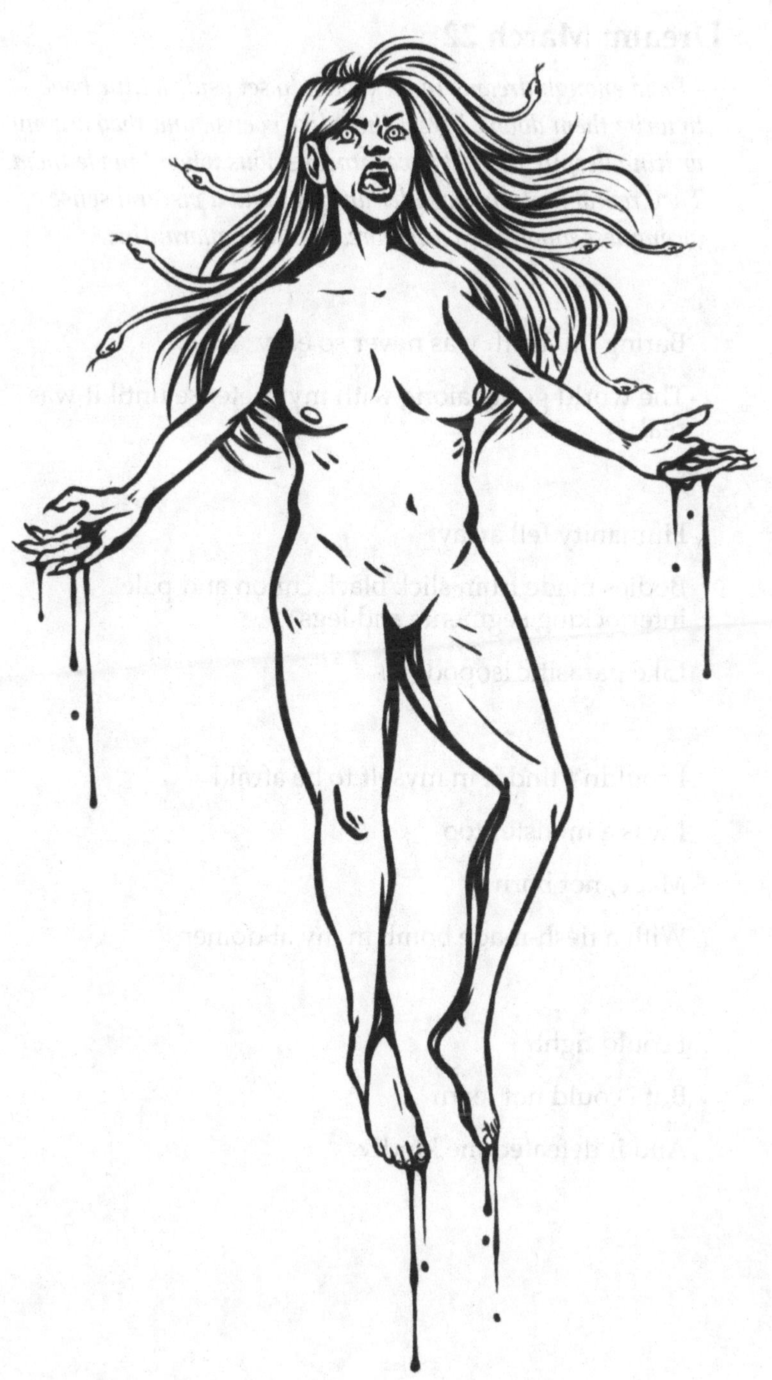

Dream: March 22

*- I had enough dreams in lockdown to set aside a little book
to write them down. I treat them like poetry, and they are my
writing despite the fact I was unconscious when I made them.
They reveal an inner wonder and fear and a visceral sense of
wrongness among the unmoored panic of quarantine.*

Baring my teeth was never so easy

The world going along with my pretense until it was
real

Humanity fell away

Bodies made from slick black chiton and pale
interlocking segments and legs

Like parasitic isopods

I couldn't find it in myself to be afraid

I was a monster too

Made, not born

With a flesh-made bomb in my abdomen

I could fight

But i could not learn

And it defeated me kindly.

Power Fantasies

March 2020

- Don't touch me.

In male power fantasies it is:

"I can do anything I want."

In female power fantasies it is:

"NO ONE CAN DO ANYTHING TO ME."

Dream: March 31

-My little sister was so intrigued by this imagery she drew a picture of the wolf - she thinks of these things in the same light as me, a sense of art and wonder where horror should be.

I was walking beside a wall.

I knew danger was a possibility.

But I had seen the great wrought-iron bars of the gate and had imagined the wolves scrabbling against it, unable to cross.

I did not know there was another sort about.

He came through the gate just out of my line of sight, pushed it, crashing, to the ground.

It was a wolf, but not.

Made from stitched leather, one head for devouring and other to laugh.

He devoured me, faster than any wolf should.

His mouth opened like a sac over my head, slipping closed.

And that was the end of it.

Sketchbook Scribbles

March and April 2020

- Snapshots from my sketchbook, most written in backwards cursive...like I said, I'm never going back.

I think I'm ok.

I'm living from moment to moment.

But each moment is a bit more of a disappointment...

Anytime I have a moment to think, alone with my monstrous thoughts, I suffer in endless spirals of uncertainty.

I'm still laughing,

Still breathing

But it isn't right.

--

Is this all there is? Is this all I have to look forward to? I think I want this to be over until someone else says it.

I'm not in hell but this must be purgatory: not loving my life, unwilling to die.

I don't know who that person in the mirror is – I think I might hate her. But I don't know if I care enough to hate her. Maybe this is just disgust.

--

Where did I go?

Because I'm not here anymore.

My body is here, every once and a while I remember to smile, to react, on instinct…but my presence here has so little effect on my emotions.

No anger.

No joy.

Where did I go?

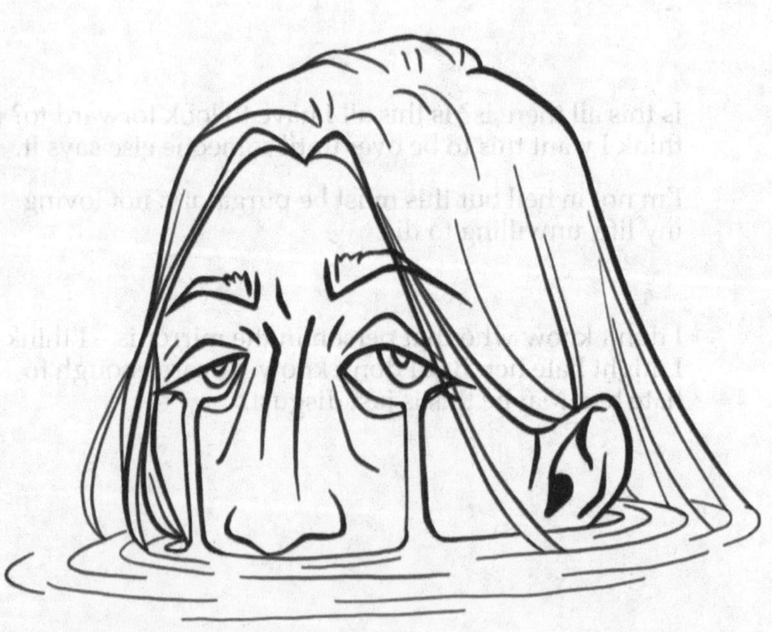

A Story Doesn't Start In Your Head
April 2020

-An old sentiment, but better articulated, I think.

A story doesn't start in your head

That's the thing about stories

They start in your emotions in that far away feeling
after dark dreams

In the anger you cannot express

In the affection you choose not to give

In the love you can't fully feel

In the loneliness that consumes you unexpectedly

Then they inhabit your body

On those nights when the sky is greying and
something in your body is full

Not full like after a meal, not content

Filled to bursting

A distracting, fluttering something in your fingers

A gnawing in your ribs

But stories escape through your brain

And that's the hard part

You have to draw them slowly from your bones

Untangle them from down in your capillaries

And sometimes they don't come out right

Sometimes you aren't careful enough

You pull too quickly

And break off the fine roots

But a story is more resilient than a plant

You can go fishing in your soul for those missing pieces

And sometimes they fit back together

But they have to come out through your brain

Even in those full times

The buzzing times

When your fingers dance

Your brain must form order from chaos

And that is the most difficult art of humanity

We do it though

One piece at a time

We have to

Our bodies can only hold so much

Dream: April 29

-Undeath and narrative and detached horror - a theme with these things - I wouldn't consider my dreams nightmares.

There was a gaggle of us who didn't matter, white and rich and adventurous, like the characters of an Agatha Christie.

We went down the river in boats at first, and there was a universal assumption, which should have bothered us, that only one of us would come back.

I jumped up onto an overhanging bridge after the young rich wife (y'know, the one on a "team" with her new husband). Yet, it couldn't have been me, the way I flipped up to her position, the way I pushed her from her seat and watched her head crack on concrete and fall into the river. I don't know if the others knew, they didn't care if they did.

I'm losing it now, but there was an island next, and a house, an old, rotting, beautiful house. What drew us there, what purpose we were meant to accomplish, I don't know. But we had luggage full of the things we might need with monogrammed name plates.

It was hard to walk in there, and days passed in minutes. I stayed in the den, listening to the house shake with violence.

The old man who came in with me had left his things in the den, and when he came back for them his throat was cut. His face was pale and his eyes were dead, the limp flap of his skin pouring blood down his waistcoat, but he came towards me with purpose.

I was afraid then, like I hadn't been before.

Every step stumbled and I left all I had behind but I made it out.

I made it only to be found by the body of the wife I had pushed in the river - white and bloated.

I ran back and forth like a child trapped in a game, mortal terror gripping my legs.

Then it was over, some unheard bell struck, and it was as if we had been playing pretend.

The man with the cut throat went back to the boat and when I asked him if he'd like his luggage, he brushed the notion aside.

Perhaps I should have taken that as a sign not to go back in the house.

I gave no thought to all that had been, or where the others were. I had seen books in there, old books. I knew there was time before the house came back to life, yet I cut the hour too close.

Just when I wanted to leave, my sister was on the boat reminding me I had left my things in the house. And I went back, of course I went back, everything important was in that backpack. (And it *was* a backpack, as if my sister's presence had drawn me out of the period piece.)

But something rose up before I could leave the house. The sun set, and a ghostly visage of a horse tried to bite at my heels.

I made it out, but the horse followed, given physical form. Its mouth gaped and its black flesh moved and cracked like plastic.

I hit it with whatever I had, and it yielded, it bloodied like a real animal, yet its pursuit of me was unbearable and unnatural. I found a chair and finished it with that. The metal cracked and cracked and cracked, bone and blood, until the body of the horse was lying still on the beach.

I couldn't see the house anymore, only the jungle, but I knew it was there.

I dug in the sand, hoping for something, like it had been the entire purpose of this journey. I did not find it.

I woke, and still I did not find it.

Comfortable

April 2020

- Maybe sentience was a mistake.

Sometimes I think my body isn't made to rest.

I watch my cat sleep,

Her soft form curls perfectly into itself, the side of her face against the blanket,

And I think,

What I wouldn't give to be that comfortable.

But no matter what I do, no matter how comfortable I think I am,

The next moment it isn't enough.

What is it about the human body?

Were we made only for thinking?

For moving?

For going at a painful, average pace until our strength
gives out?

I think if we could sleep like cats - our own bodies like
small pillows - we'd sleep forever

And civilization would peacefully crumble.

What I wouldn't give to be that comfortable,

That at peace.

Would I trade enlightenment for the quiet…?

Maybe.

Knowing has only ever brought me pain.

It's what they don't tell you about the mountain top.

Once you get there,

It sucks.

Quieter Than It Should Be

May 15, 2020

- The night before my birthday.

Most breakdowns are quieter than they should be.

<<I'm living one panicked moment to another, but I'm a big girl now>>

I tried to see if it was possible to break my skin with my fingernails,

Mistook the tears on my arm for blood and felt foolish.

The walls here are so thin but no one can hear me crying

<<Then again, I don't interfere when I hear someone else's tears>>

I can't tell if I'm broken or if pain is the human condition.

Doesn't everyone hurt themselves sometimes?

The Best of Summer
June 26, 2020

- I try to find the beauty in each season, but I'm partial to this.

I saw the eagles flying away from that oncoming cloud,

But I stood still,

Ignoring the itch of biting insects at my ankles.

I was enraptured, held still by the heavy air.

The sun cast gold and blushing hues on the face of the storm, whispering pink mammatus hurrying away and the horizon stained like a summer dress.

The birds stayed sitting in whatever roosts they could find, scarcely disturbed by my presence. A herd of deer moved nervously forward, nibbling as they went, picturesque in that altered light.

But I stood still.

The rumbling voice of the storm came ever closer, lecturing almost, in a continuous drone. It shakes beneath my feet and I do not care if I don't know what it says. I listen anyway.

Only the lightning bugs go on as usual. Or perhaps with more vigor, dancing before the flashes of the storm like they had seen the face of their god.

When I leave, I walk backwards, moved as the hot heavy air of waiting is pushed aside, and I can smell the rain on the growing wind.

Still, I am sorry to go inside.

The best of summer, to be caught between an oncoming thunderstorm and the sunset, heedless of the mosquitoes.

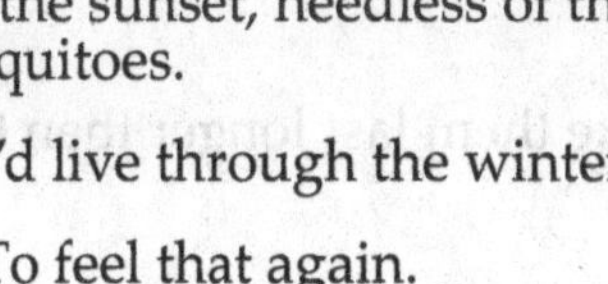

I'd live through the winter.

To feel that again.

Smell of Death
June 7, 2020

- I collect bird skulls and bones - the culmination of a long project.

I can't get the smell of death off my hands.

It was only a few hours I spent in the rot, but it sank into my skin somehow.

I can't bring myself to mind.

There are some smells that are only unpleasant in larger quantities, and it feels like a reminder somehow.

It doesn't bring me horror anymore,

     Even if some primal part of me knows that the smell and the squelch can be dangerous,

It is only a process.

I sink into it,

Disappear for a while.

Peeling back skin and prying out what used to be eyes, wiping off the wetness that was neural tissue a long time ago,

It doesn't disgust me like it should.

The carrion flies keep me company, the ants around my knees,

They know it too.

     It is only a process.

And I do not pity the organisms that once owned these hollow shells.

It feels good to make them last longer than they would have,

To cherish the shapes of them,

To teach others that bones are only future dirt.

I don't think I would mind someone doing the same to my skull.

I'm not using it anymore.

The smell still clings to my skin, though,

Despite the gloves and the tools.

I use three kinds of soap to deaden it, driven by some distant voice that reminds me that my skin is supposed to protect me.

But you cannot kill death.

It is only a process.

You can only accept it, and clean the remains.

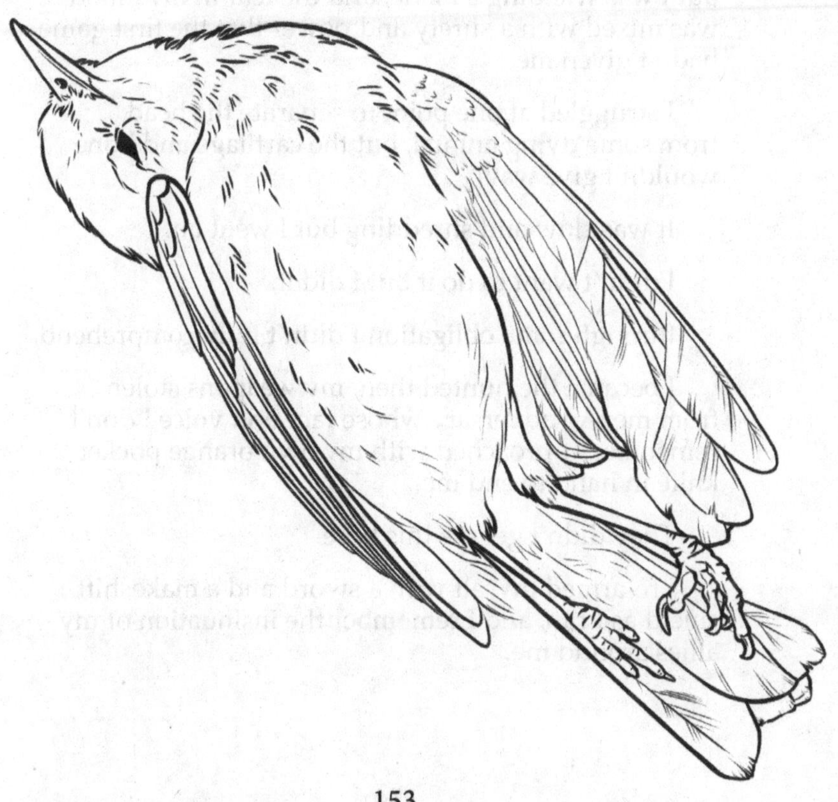

Dream: July 5

*-I always feel like I'm playing along in a game I pretend to
understand.*

It was a ritual I understood but had never done,
joining the crowd and hoping no one would see me as
a fraud.

I didn't want to do it but I did it,

through some obligation I didn't fully comprehend.

I was annoyed, and maybe angry.

We were in shallow water, on a timer, and the
sweep of a searchlight changed the game.

I don't remember why, don't remember the rules,
but I was wielding a blade, and the fear in my blood
was mixed with a surety and power that the first game
hadn't given me.

I struggled at one point to separate the head
from some dying animal, but the cartilage and bone
wouldn't give way.

It was slow and shredding but I went on.

I didn't want to do it but I did it,

through some obligation I didn't fully comprehend.

I became the hunted then, my weapons stolen
from me. An adversary whose face and voice I don't
remember approached with my own orange pocket
knife in hand to end me.

They didn't get me this time.

I re-armed myself with a sword and a makeshift
shield as I ran, and I remember the insinuation of my
allies around me.

I did not find my adversary again.

I do not remember how it ended.

But no one touched me.
No one breached my skin.

[New Apartment]

Dream: August 19

-I'm wiser in my sleep.

I dreamt I was a tanuki,

    A tiger.

I said,

    "Choose the right time to fight, and fight fiercely."

Dream: August 26

-My sister and I make our confrontations in our dreams - we scream silently for now.

I dreamt I got a tattoo of a dolphin in a spaceship, brightly colored, at the base of my neck.

It's not something I would have wanted in real life, but in a dream, who can account for taste.

There was a handsome bearded man that did it for me, and it wasn't quite what I wanted but I thanked him anyway.

We snuck into his house with my parents, I don't remember why, and we found old cabinets full of books before he came home and welcomed us as if we were friends. M_____ was with me through all of this, of course she was.

When the towel on my neck dried and I took the paper off from beneath it, my skin peeled. I told them it was fine, I'd been hurt worse, and I did it myself.

I scooted over the floor to show my mom, pulled back my hair. She had nothing good to say, only mild criticisms and questions. In that space of the dream I asked her why, why couldn't she just be happy for me, why couldn't she support my decision. I didn't show the tattoo to dad.

She was quiet in the aftermath. Not chastised, only pretending to be the better person, to put me down by being "reasonable."

We drove back home on a wide, dry highway full of construction, and she tried to tell me that I was under her authority. That I, her 23 year old daughter, should have gotten her approval for this type of decision. I told her I was under God's authority and no one else's, and when she repeated what I said I replied simply, "Yep."

And that was the end of it, a sour taste in my mouth when I woke.

First Day of School

-Our shadows have shadows,

We Aren't White

August 2020

- I will never not be furious.

We aren't white.

I'd like to hurt whoever called us white,

      Whoever had the blindness to call us an ideal.

White is the combination of every color,

        While we have only ever been a lack,

          A translucence.

A half-mottled mix of tints where melanocytes never grew.

We're just narrow jaws and crooked teeth,

      Pink and purple stretch marks where we couldn't fit in our own skin.

We aren't white.

      We're pink - blood flushed at our fingertips and in our faces, an ugly texture, every imperfection showing, so easily disturbed.

We aren't white.

      We're green and purple and blue,

        The hazy paths where veins show through.

I'm not saying we're to be pitied,

or, god-forbid,

oppressed.

But I'm disgusted.
I've got no culture beyond supremacy,
And it makes me damn depressed.

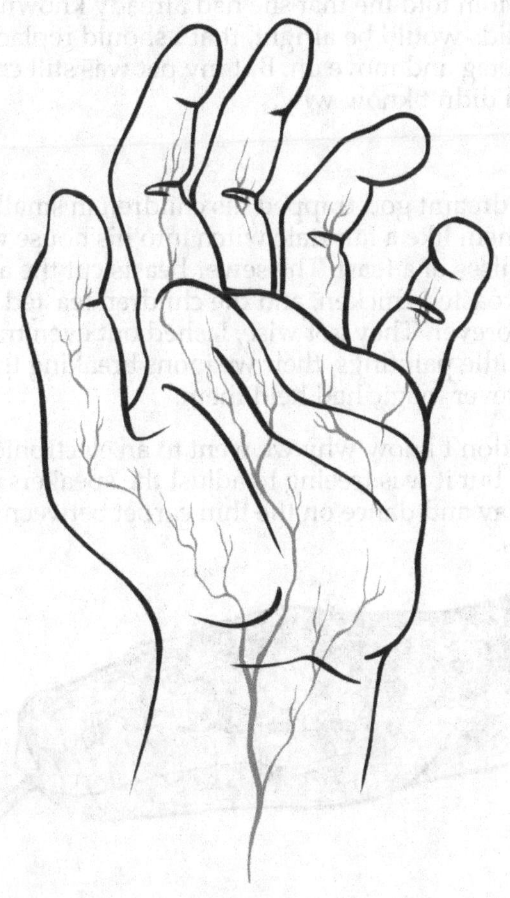

Dream: September 25

-Suki is my Carpet Python, one of many pets that only some would have the taste to cherish.

I dreamt that I held Suki up in my hands, my beloved little monster. She was shorter than she should have been, missing part of herself. I realized suddenly that though she was still crawling around my hands, she'd been dead for a while. The bottom of her body returned and reattached, her tiny ribs crawling like insect legs and I've never been afraid of her but I backed away then in real horror and grief.

Mom told me that she had already known, that the kids would be alright, that I should replace her nametag and move on. But my pet was still crawling and I didn't know why.

-

I dreamt god trapped his children in small objects, led them like a fairytale witch into his house with promises of a feast. The sewer beasts cut the apples and roasted chicken, and the children feasted but not forever. They got wise, lashed out even trapped like little paintings, their weapons breaking through whatever magic had held them.

I don't know why we went to an electronics store next, but it was freeing to adjust the speakers on display and dance on the thin carpet between the aisles.

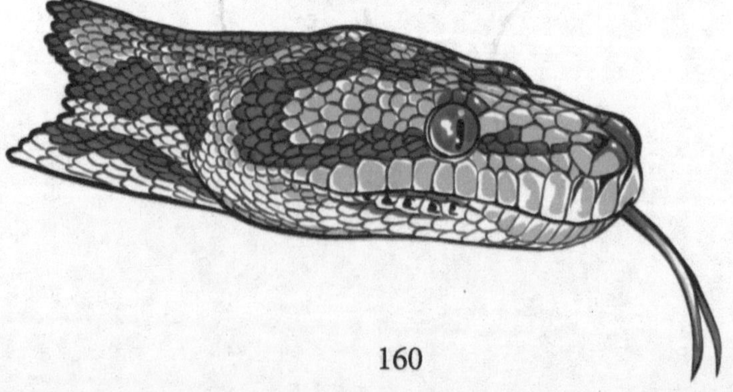

Oh Lord My God

September 2020

- Religious deconstruction sometimes comes out as parody.
(Hymns were the closest to God I got.)

Oh Lord my God, I'm lost, not understanding.

I see the price that all of us have paid.

I cannot stay, pretend it doesn't matter,

I cannot be the child my parents made.

Then sings my soul, my God how can it be?

It breaks my heart.

It breaks my heart.

Then sings my soul, my God how can it be?

It breaks my heart.

It breaks my heart.

Oh Lord my God, I feel like I've been lied to.

They use your words, to hurt, to cast aside.

They close their fists, no matter the intention,

Unchanging hearts, blinded by their pride.

Then sings my soul, my God how can it be?

It breaks my heart.

It breaks my heart.

Then screams my soul, my God how can it be?

It breaks my heart.

It breaks my heart.

Dream: September 26

-One of those I wish I could remember better - I like stories

I dreamt of riding horses, of debts and magic and tricks and games.

I was someone greater than I am, still not quite a hero.

It felt like a grand story but I only remember fragments.

There was an old man, at first a threat (a whisper of an old power) but revealed to be a trick...at least, if his power was real, he didn't hurt me.

There was a relic of light he carried with him that cast shapes and runes on the walls in purple and blue and green. (It was the relic that was the real power, a living light.)

The old man was searching for his wife, and I took him out of solitude to a little cantina to find her. I couldn't see his face when they met again, but they did not embrace, and I'm still not sure I did any good.

I went on.

I lost the light. I was trapped in an electric fence with horses that wanted to trample me, but I did not die. I rode them, took the largest one as my escape.

I went on.

I got to an arena, willingly or not I don't remember. I lost the fight, again and again, to the wolves, but I did not die. I sat defeated in the center of the arena with the bloodless fragments of my steed around me.

I was given a reward for my performance (for my failure). It looked like a single nugget of gold, but it was warm, and it stretched like a caramel candy until I could see what was trapped inside it, until the gold was a porthole view of a horse made of gold and fire.

Breakup Songs
September 2020

- Mourning myself.

This is for those of us
who cry at break up songs,
mourning nothing.

Repressed and afraid, our own
inclinations made into demons, every
experience and life lesson we've been told
we should have had stolen from us.

And every story, every song

       Is about something we've never had.

Never lost a connection, never had one,

       Lost

             Wondering if we're unlovable or broken.

         (Wondering if I'm a sociopath or just annoying)

We ruin every chance we get, tripped by the
expectation that we know what to do, what to say…

I don't have time to reclaim my youth, too consumed
by survival to seek out connection until I look around
again and I'm alone.

We cry over love songs too, at the idea of forever.

Still,

Can't lose what we never had.

(I say we out of hope that I'm not the only one.)

Dream: September 29

-That feeling of needing to run but being unable to move - I feel it awake and asleep

I dreamt I was climbing up a hill in heels, red ones I would never wear in waking. I was looking for someone, I don't remember who. There was a gift shop at the top of it. I remember going through it, disgusted that it was nothing more than meaningless plastic and useless, craftless tchotchkes, and disgusted with myself for thinking it would be something more, for hoping.

I didn't find what I was looking for, I spent too long trying to get past an obstacle, a piece of ground covered in several rotting animals heaped together entirely by accident. I was trying to get around them, up the hill, trying to avoid the swarming carrion bugs and soupy detritus. It was then that one body stood up from the rest, a little goat kid. He had been lying too long atop the protruding vertebrae of a deer, open sores down his chest. I don't know what made him stand, what made him live, but he bounded towards me uncaring for his broken, filthy body, still full of that wriggling, butting energy that is so familiar to me. He looked just like one of that first pair of goats we bottle-fed, little Pete, so pretty and joyful and wounded.

I could respond to him with only horror and confusion, not sure what to do, how to help. The dream did not resolve, but I know Pete lives in Minnesota now, and the dead stay rotting.

Dream: October 9

-The first time I dreamt about my students - but not the last.

I dreamt I was dealing with a child, like I do every day now. And she was willful. She didn't understand I was trying to protect her.

She had two box cutters, one gripped in each hand, extending their blades and dragging them across my skin, cutting my hands when I tried to take them away.

Only two of the wounds bled, even then, shallower than that sort of wound should have. I did not cry out, and I got the blades away, put them in books and out of her reach.

I stared at the scratches even as I tried to get her to bed, already coagulating.

The child whined.

She wanted her blades back.

Dream: October 10

-Can't you just believe me when I say I know what I'm talking about?

I dreamt a good many things, but there is only a fragment I remember.

More than once I was bitten by one of my snakes, little teeth sinking in over and over. It upsets me that they would think I could hurt them.

I was waiting in line. I was questioned (my profession, my purpose) by a nagging voice that knew nothing of me but that I was me, and I was bitten.

Dream: November 13

-Always together: nostalgia and disgust.

I was meant to house-sit.

It was a little place, far out in the country and built halfway into the hillside.

It had an oldness to it that was both familiar and uncomfortable, filled with musty, ugly furniture I could not change, and concrete basement walls I could not paint.

It should have felt empty, but where there should have been people there was a silent fullness, a haunted bitterness at being abandoned, and I dreaded trying to sleep on that green plaid couch.

The house was terrible, but it took up space in a lovely rolling plain.

I remember clearly seeing a stand of tall wildflowers, burning orange, and wanting in the dream to take a picture to keep that vision forever.

But I never did.

Dream: November 21

-They look to me but I'm not sure either.

We were rebels, conspirators, past failures, barely more than children.

We seemed only half human, trading body parts for smuggled half-formed wings, surviving the cold and the scarcity.

We were meant to gather resources, hiding things away from our overlords.

The tyrant was lazy and sloppy, our poorly accomplished clandestiny slipping under his nose. With me between him and them, the only one really giving orders.

I was the queen of crows but I could not fly.

Dream: December 15

-Fight to preserve - to undo mistakes - but time goes on - and rot is not undone.

I was back at college, taking care of animals that weren't mine, surrounded by carefully preserved and categorized death.

The professor came to ask after his rat and it came as a shock to me when I bent down to the cage and found only bleach-white rodent bones

I tried to apologize, my tongue stuck in my throat, but the professor seemed almost unbothered, as if expecting my failure. He walked away with a sad shake of his head, and that was worse than anger.

I was trying to teach then, in the casual sense that I used to in the hallways, when I saw movement along the shelves - a twisting of one preserved, desiccated body. It was a snake, a scrub python maybe, skin dried to its ribs and crawling away.

[I'm starting to wonder about how often this year I've dreamt of undeath]

I don't know how long I spent chasing that snake, trying to find somewhere to put him, but there is nowhere a creature like that can belong.

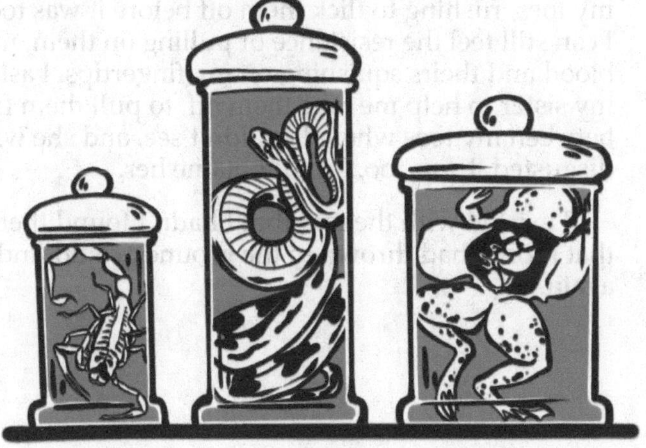

2021
(Renovation)

I try to make myself into something I can love. It's still a work in progress, it always will be, but I'm trying.

Age: 24

Dream: January 20

-I could do without this sense memory

It was a blur of confusion and aversion but the part I remember best was the ticks.

Someone had slipped them into my clothes, a joke or a cruelty, it didn't really matter.

I can still see them crawling over my skin, between my toes, rushing to flick them off before it was too late. I can still feel the resistance of pulling on them, my blood and theirs squishing on my fingertips. I asked my sister to help me take them off, to pull them from between my toes where I couldn't see, and she was disgusted. I was too, I didn't blame her.

I existed with the fear that I hadn't found them all, that those I had thrown to the ground would find me again.

Dream: February 23

-I don't remember this one now, but it must be mine.

I only remember the smuggling and the maggots, the gurgling boat with which we were meant to cross the river.

That, and the Spinosaurus behind a wall of water, the river held up like the Jordan, towering like the ancient teeth within it. All manner of beautiful monsters I will never get the chance to really see. When they lunged towards the barrier there was panic in my chest, but a smile on my face.

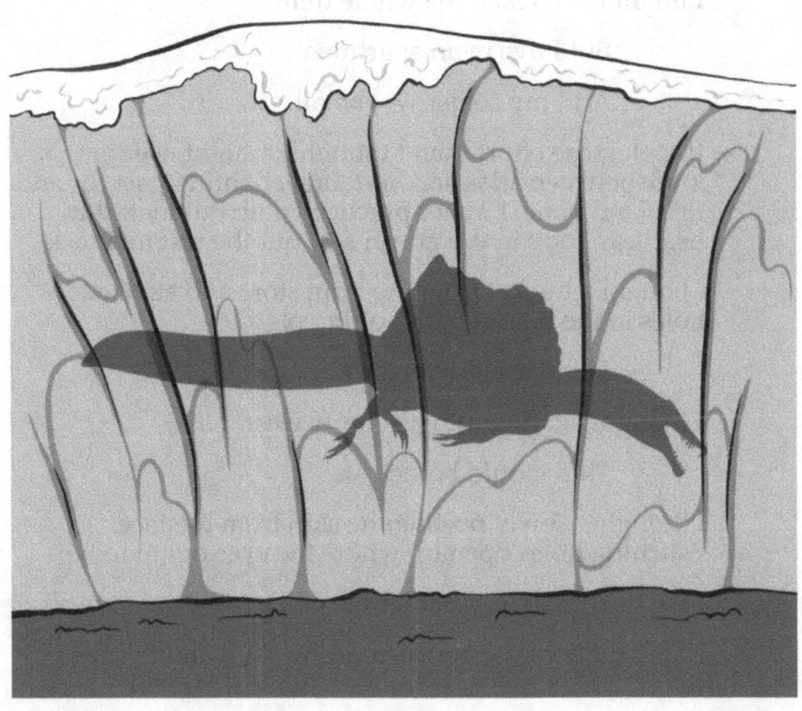

It Should Have Bothered Me

March 2021

- What it says on the box.

It should have bothered me,

    Cutting the head from that raccoon

But it was dead,

    And it was free,

        And I hate to see anything go to waste.

"Gettin' that raccoon?" the man in the truck asked me, noticing my hazard lights, a young woman standing alone on the side of the road.

"Yep." Was all I said, standing in sturdy boots with a knife in my hand watching him drive away.

I might have taken the whole thing,

    But I live in an apartment,

    And my cooler was small.

It took more effort than I thought it might, wedging my knife between atlas and vertebrae, fighting past fur and flesh and bone. I'm not practiced at it. But I left that headless body in the gravel and put the rest in a sack.

I bought a bucket from the farm store and stabbed holes in the lid, my little rotting place.

    This should bother me

I thought, staring into its empty eyes

    This should bother me

I thought, slowly peeling the skin from the face, watching holes open up where the eyes ought to be

    This should bother me

I thought, looking between fleshy skull and fleshless hide

This should bother me

I thought, slicing shreds of red meat from planes of its broken jaw and leaving them in a plastic grocery bag.

This should bother me

I thought, watching black ichor leak from its eyes.

This should bother me

I thought, cutting out its white tongue.

This should bother me

But it didn't.

There was no smell like before.

Just me and the newly dead.

Just me and the shattered back of the cranium where the brain was beginning to leak.

Just me and the chill of early spring and the noise of my neighbors on the balcony above me.

Just the pull of the knife and the laughter in my headphones.

Just the dead.

Just tomorrow.

Dream: March 13

-Two parts. I lost what fit between them.

It was a small place, presided over by a cursed sort of man with a long stride and generous hands. He kept animals on the top of the hill, moving from building to building through the drifted snow, but he loved the kittens best.

It was town hall and church both, grander when the host was in it, the resting place of the speaking horn. The ghosts in the rafters printed newspapers for the town and the ungrateful went home hungry.

-

The end of the dream had me trying to navigate a city, plastic on the wind, lost and frustrated with a group of people who might have been my family but weren't.

I was supposed to go back to college, stepping back into a classroom full of fish tanks with a professor I knew to be a botanist, and the weight of all the decisions I needed to make was suffocating.

I didn't want to work at Best Buy.

I didn't want to live on campus.

E___ didn't want to room with me.

Notes App: March 18, 2021, 2:28 PM

-Amazing the way Notes can catalog the specificity of these thoughts - hold them like fossilized amber.

If I type on this will I look busy?

Will they see the unfocused haze in my eyes?

I am surrounded by children and fools too consumed by the American Monstrosity to see the monolithic horror that is this new world.

I don't want to die.

I don't think so.

I just want to sleep.

I just want to be
in the quiet and
darkness for a while,
pardoned from the
responsibilities of
existence, of paying and
insisting on paying for
the mistakes of those who
came before me.

I just want to lie down
without feeling the
desperate sound of my
own heartbeat.

Is this how it's supposed to feel?
I'm so tired.

I Knew

March 2020

- I give my snakes cute names but their loss feels like anything but.

He was only a little animal,

Insignificant in the scheme of time and the monstrosity of Life,

But he was mine.

I don't know that he ever liked me much,

But I loved him.

His keeper and his killer.

I never thought I would stoop to neglect.

(Not after the childhood I've had)

The villain and the victim.

My irresponsibility ripping this small thing that I loved from the arms of my inner child.

And

I knew

I knew

I knew

I knew two days before when he wandered weak and wasted in my hand.

I knew when I threw away that pinkie mouse after one
last attempt to feed him.

I knew when I put the sign over his cage that said not
to bother him.

I knew within my sickness that was forcing me away.

I smelled it when I walked in the room,

Endured it though the whole day,

      Postponing my grief with feigned ignorance
and a cardboard hope.

I knew…

I always know.

Anxious prophetess of
inevitabilities.

I'll miss you,
Snoot.

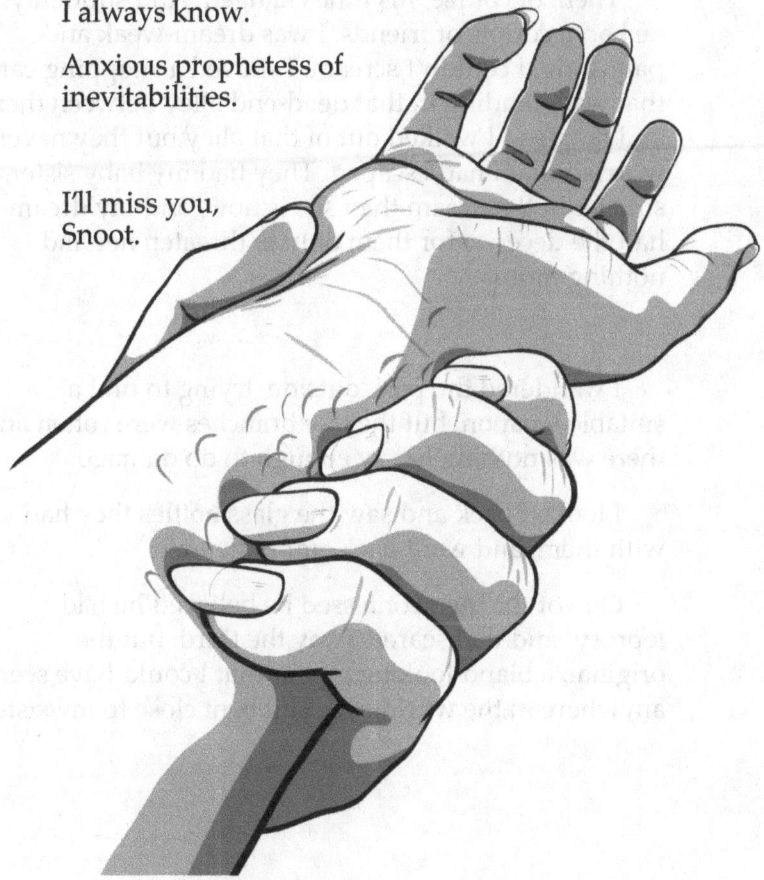

Dream: March 27

-I took action in this one - better than usual.

I was driving a semi down the narrow streets of France, trying to reach some homely destination where my family would welcome me.

A man asked if he could help me, (I should know that a man never really asks for help) and he had a proper license and an un-stolen car but he was still a stranger and I told him so.

Then, of course, his tune changed. And suddenly he had a couple of friends. I was dream-weak and panicking. I couldn't scream. I shoved a shopping cart that was standing in that dead-end alley between them and me. And I walked out of that alley but they never worried that I had escaped. They had my baby sister, smaller in the dream than she is now, and my dream had the decency for them only to threaten her and nothing more.

I wandered the park outside, trying to find a suitable weapon, but the tree branches were rotten and there was nothing heavy enough to do damage.

I looked back and saw the glass bottles they had with them, and went back empty handed.

One of the men confessed he believed he had leprosy, and that scared away the third, but the original, a bland looking ginger that I could have seen anywhere in the world, was still bent close to my sister.

He did little but watch me when I took the bottle and smashed the end on the concrete. Did nothing when I buried it in his companion's head, when his skull caved in like it was glass as well.

It cut my thumb nail.

I got O______ back, though she had never been herself in the dream, a limp doll of a thing I cared about, but I think I won.

Nothing happened to that bland-faced ginger.

Triggered

- "My generation." As if that means anything besides the disadvantaged masses.

My unwillingness to be stepped on is not a weakness.

So, stop calling me

    "Sensitive"

    And

    "Triggered"

When you're the one holding the gun.

Thought

March 2021

- Those wordless nights when I've spent too long in the shower and fall into myself, who else is there to talk to?

I wonder sometimes how thought works for everyone else.

    Wonder if it ever goes away…

For me.

    It is…an ocean…a shadow…

        …fanning out forever behind me…

          (only ever behind me)

There is always something lingering, behind the
surface of my consideration,

> Layers dimming

>> Towards something I cannot touch.

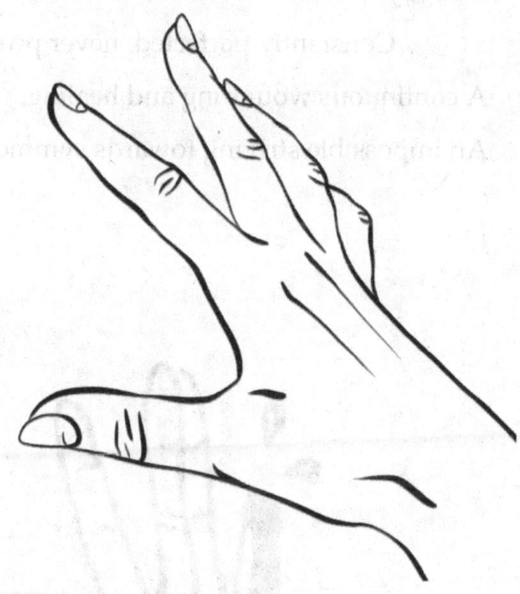

I coax it forward as I fall asleep

> With stories and images and unfelt sensations

>> (wings unfurling)

Currents and eddies and plans over some depth I will
never measure.

> I'm not making some grand creature of myself.

I only know that I fall – staring forward – and the deep
surges up.

Like My Nails

-I don't bite them but I don't know if this is better.

Like my nails,

Constantly perfected, never properly cared for,

A continuous wounding and healing,

An impossible striving towards symmetry.

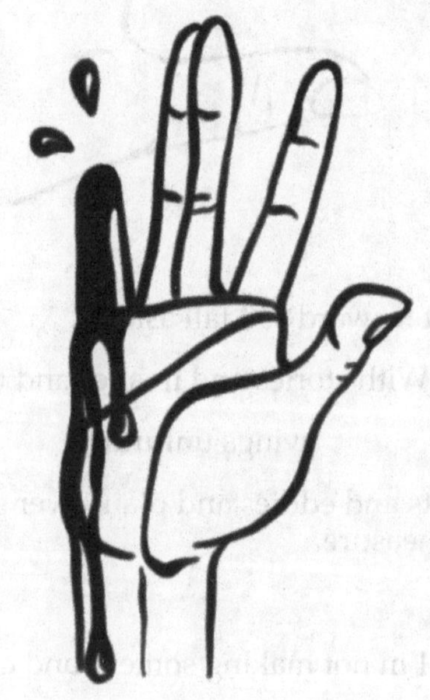

Almost Missed the Moon

March 2021

- I will never grow out of a love for the night, for the stars, for Her.

I almost missed the moon tonight,

Caught between exhaustion and worry, turning off the lights.

I could see her then, in the moment before I turned away, low and yellow and

     I gasped

     (because it will always be like the first time)

Just a shadow sliver along a gibbous, hovering between the ugly architecture of this nothing town.

My mind has still been caught in winter,

frozen and depressed by the weight of snow,

so caught up in my own misery I forget to look around.

I hadn't noticed the yellow moon or the soft breeze. I hadn't noticed the call of frogs for the first time since the thaw, and it brought tears to my eyes.

     I notice now.

     I've noticed now.

This is what I mean when I say I love the seasons.

Even the streetlight that allows me to scarcely see my paper seems a shame, seems blasphemous.

Someday, I'll move into the country and worship the night as she ought to be.

The moon's risen past the telephone tower now, and the frogs will sing until summer fades to fall.

I'm sure my handwriting is atrocious, not enough light to see anything but the inclination of what has been written, nothing to enforce or indulge my perfectionism.

Perhaps it is a good thing.

I can see the big dipper from my balcony and this wind is from the South.

It doesn't feel like a Fool's Spring this time.

    I am allowed to hope.

        To sing like frogs at the yellow moon and herald night.

I go to bed a little fuller.

Just Don't

April 2021

- The spiraling aftermath of an "inspirational speech" given to new teachers by a colleague.

Just Don't.

Don't tell me another fucking story

About a millionaire who didn't used to be.

Maybe I'm a disillusioned cynic,

Maybe I'm enlightened,

I'm not sure there's a difference.

But I'm not going to be Oprah,

And I don't care if Michael Jordan lost a bunch of games,

And I'd tear out my tongue before proclaiming Disney a role model (that racist monopoly of a rat king).

Give me a fucking break.

Do you all actually believe this shit?

That adversity is something to be proud of?

Why don't you just admit that the system's a failure?

Why not just admit we're doing nothing but surviving?

Don't praise me for my resilience when my pain was
unnecessary.

I'm an idealist.

But not that kind (not that way).

I can't spread my ideas over bland white toast for your
pleasure.

   (You wouldn't like the way the truth tastes.)

I'm an idealist, but not one with the blind hope you
seem to cling to.

   (I think my brain would burn you if it leaked
from my skull.)

This pain is acidic.

But it's only human.

Please stop pretending you don't feel it too

'cause they'll keep on telling these tales

And you should know it'll never be you.

It's systemic.

It's society.

It's not you.

It's not me.

But we can't fight the beast together if you won't
acknowledge the teeth crushing your ribs.

Don't tell me,

  A teacher,

(chronically underpaid)

That this rough start is something I have in common
with the stars.

(I have it in common with the scum too.)

We glorify breaking ourselves for a broken system and
I'm sick of it.

Don't tell me another fucking inspirational story.

(I'm not Steve Jobs – thank the stars for that – and he
didn't start Apple with just a fucking garage)

Just Don't.

Don't talk to me about hope until you've looked this
beast in the mouth.
Don't try to change my mind.

I'd rather be a cynic than a fool.

Notes App: May 20, 2021, 2:47 PM

-I hate seeing the beginnings of wrinkles on my face but the feeling persists.

So much to do

So little time

It's what they always tell you about getting older

But no young person ever believes it

A little wiser every day

Every day a little more desperate

I'm already so tired, I don't know how I could do this for longer but what else is there

This existence I will never understand

  -that thing which sends my mind into a panicked spiral when I consider it too much, when I feel like I can't escape my own face-

  It's all there is

    All that I know there is to be

All my joys and pains wrapped up in this…

  Whatever this is

I used to be sure of what I was and where I was going

Notes App: May 27, 2021, 12:24 PM

*-My students accidentally saw the title of this one and
laughed, I am glad they could not see the rest.*

Today is rainy.

I wish that I could be napping, listening to the poetic
drumming on the windows,

Wrapped in the heavy air, warm and wet with spring.

I was born in this month, and I feel as if it's left a mark
on me.

I am most at peace in a late spring storm, watching
the green things return, the warm wind and the sun
through the infant leaves.

I wonder if the poetry's left
me.

I'm just stating things now,
little left of the analogy that
used to be easy, the weight
my words used to have.

Today is grey.

And I have to go on
working, ignoring the
inner landscape of my
eyelids which calls to
me.

I am always pretending.

Today, I am pretending to be here.

I Keep Buying Plants

June 2021

- The cycles of hope and disappointment. (The pumping of my heart.)

I keep buying plants.

They bring life to my gloomy, scholarly interior, to my collection of death.

It is something I feel like I need, refusing to remember that I spend nearly all my hours in a wood and concrete box.

They keep dying.

I'm not completely well these days, I do not do what I need or what I want.

The guilt I feel when I realize the brown edges have crept farther is hard to ignore.

Sometimes – oftentimes – it is too late.

There are a few that hold on, that have stayed with me in the spirit of stubbornness that is all life, despite not being cared for properly. It will hurt the most when they go.

There is an analogy here somewhere for the way I care for myself (reactionary) – for my own brown-leaf existence.

There is an analogy here somewhere for my sense of hope, the cycle of plans and growth and disappointment I will not learn from.

I'm jaded certainly, sometimes I think I'm beyond hope.

But I keep buying plants.

Dunkin Donuts Bag

June 2021

*- I wish someone would tell me if this is what executive
dysfunction is.*

I left a dead pheasant in a Dunkin' Donuts bag on my
porch.

I'd meant to deal with it right away,

(I'd stolen it from the road in a moment of passion)

To cut off its head, pluck a few feathers and feed the
rest back to the ditch.

.

But it's still there…

.

Best laid plans, I guess.

But there are maggots on my porch,

And a black spot I'm hoping washes out…

It smells a bit…

Maybe it's depression, maybe something else.

Probably executive dysfunction over laziness…

Doesn't really matter.

.

It's still a mess.

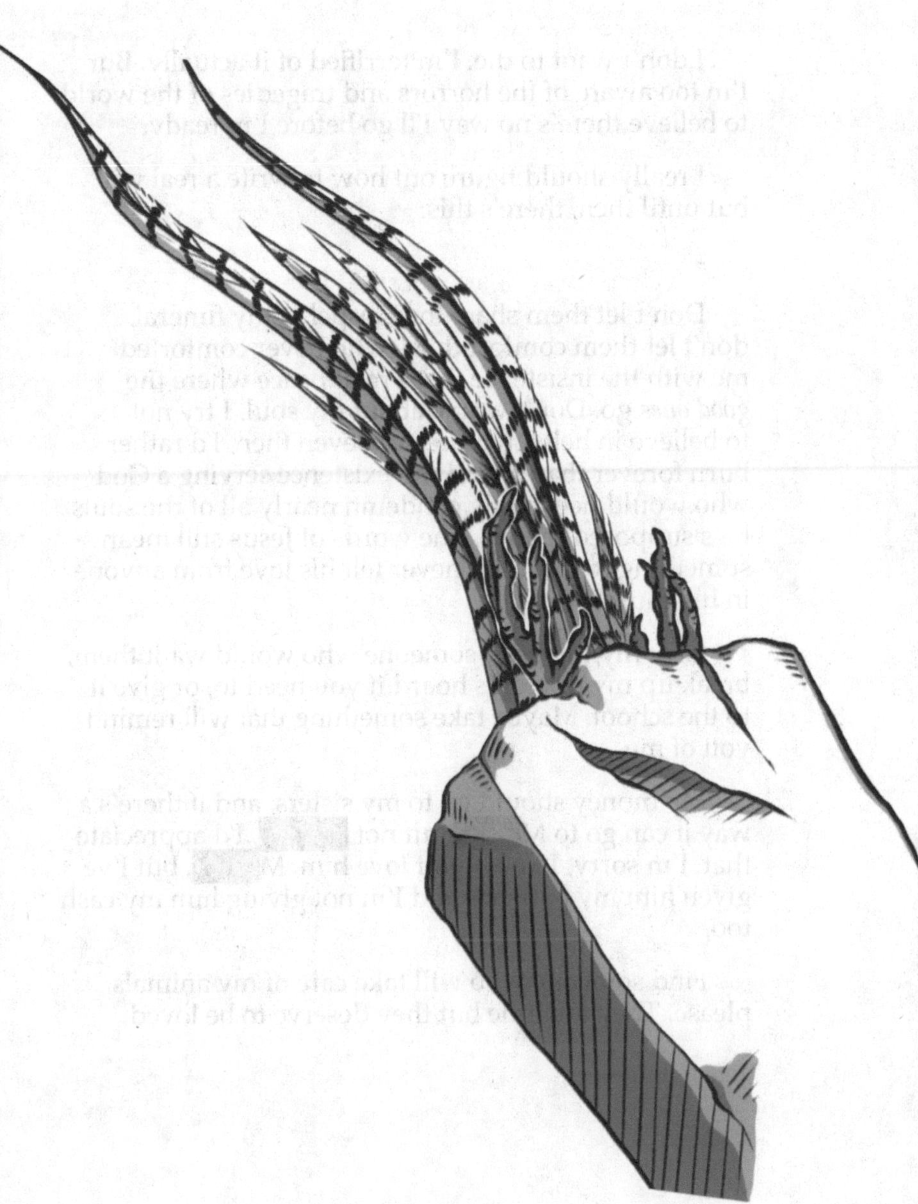

If I Die Early

-Some things aren't for publishing, but I'm unwilling to wait until I'm dead to be heard.

I don't want to die. I'm terrified of it actually. But I'm too aware of the horrors and tragedies of the world to believe there's no way I'll go before I'm ready.

I really should figure out how to write a real will, but until then, there's this.

-

Don't let them share the Gospel at my funeral, don't let them comfort those who never comforted me with the insistence that I'm at peace where the *good ones* go. Don't worry about my soul. I try not to believe in hell anymore, and even then, I'd rather burn forever than spend my existence serving a God who would needlessly condemn nearly all of the souls he's supposed to love. The words of Jesus still mean something to me, but I never felt his love from anyone in his church.

Give my things to someone who would want them, break up my dragon's hoard if you need to, or give it to the school. Maybe take something that will remind you of me.

My money should go to my sisters, and if there's a way it can go to M█████ but not ████████, I'd appreciate that. I'm sorry, I know you love him, M█████, but I've given him my patience and I'm not giving him my cash too.

Find someone who will take care of my animals please. They are little but they deserve to be loved.

-Mom-

I love you, I really do, but I've never once told you everything I really thought, and this is the one chance I'll get when you can't explain away my pain for me.

I loved you, but I feared you too.

You didn't even really know me, so if you'd like to honor my memory, don't go around acting like you did. It's been a long time since you knew what I wanted.

And while we're on the subject of honoring my memory, please find it in yourself to give my sisters the grace and humility you never had for me. You tried to encourage my interests - and I'll always be grateful for that – but you didn't listen to me, or comfort me, or believe me when I needed you to. I know it wasn't all your fault, but I'm sick of pretending that none of it was. I'm sick of pretending it doesn't hurt. It's too late to fix it. I just want you to be sorry. I'm too old to hope you'll change, but you could at least try.

I say *I love you* with the same certainty I feel when I hear it from you.

-Dad-

You never made me afraid, and for that, I love you.

You always let us have fun, and that was precious to me, but I've never really felt like you were my ally.

Keep laughing, you know I always loved your stupid jokes.

-M████-

What can I say. You're everything to me.

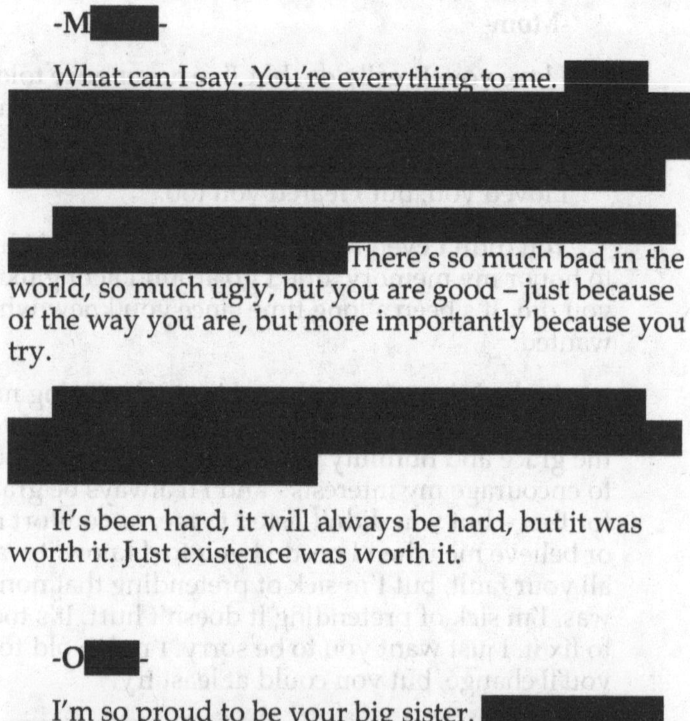

There's so much bad in the world, so much ugly, but you are good – just because of the way you are, but more importantly because you try.

It's been hard, it will always be hard, but it was worth it. Just existence was worth it.

-O███-

I'm so proud to be your big sister.

We're a lot alike, I think. Don't let them make you afraid to be yourself. Don't let them tell you that you're too old for imagination.

I really hope we only become better friends, and if we don't get the chance, know I love you more than all imaginary worlds put together.

-V███████-

I don't believe in as much as I used to, but I do wish I could believe in soulmates. You know I love that idea.

I'm so lucky to have had you, I hope you never have to read this, I hope we change together but never drift apart.

When we both said we were the kind of lonely children who always hoped for a best friend, that moved something in me.

I don't intend to leave you, but if I do, I suppose I'll meet you in the stars.

Comfort
June 2021

- Little else to say.

I take comfort in the brutal reality of nature.

It has never once lied to say that it would comfort me.

Lightning Show
June 2021

- Every summer.

There's a storm to the south alive with lightning. It will not reach me here. I can barely hear a trace of the rolling thunder as I creep away from the buildings and into the shadows along the fence line. There is too much light here, even in this nothing town, but I make due.

There are fireflies in the grass and the electricity in the sky – lightning calls to lightning, soundless, heedless of the world, heedless of me.

I could fall asleep here in the damp comfort of the summer night, but I will not.

The flashes of the lightning have been going on for hours now, there's a childish part of me that wonders if it could go on forever. I know it will not, but there is comfort in knowing there are some parts of nature that man could never drive to extinction.

Maybe it will be our downfall, forgetting these old gods...

I have not forgotten.

It feels as though I am the only one who is looking, the only one who knew they were showing fireworks tonight.

I have not forgotten.

I cannot forget.

I cannot suffer the winter without knowing this is waiting for me.

Bad Witches

June 2021

- I'm a part of academia now.

I had a dream about a magic school, one as problematic and underfunded as the real thing. I was a witch but not myself. She had all my internal audacity and anger and ideas but turned outwards. She had purple hair and spoke out of turn.

There was a punishment that was supposed to fit the crime: a transmutation which would make one ear of the offending witch large and grotesque. It was reversible, but when the student spoke the charm, the resulting transmutation was painful.

The witch which was me was not afraid, she stalked around the room with more power than I have ever felt, scolding the teacher for continuing such old, barbaric practices. She knew what I know, that punishment and social isolation does not cure bad witches but creates them.

"Why do you think there are bad witches but for this?!"

This Land
June 2021

-This feels incomplete.

This land it makes racists
This land it makes fools
This land it makes white folks
Who meanly follow rules

This land it makes commies
Out of those of us who care
This land it makes leftists
Close to pulling out their hair

This land holds its rage
In the summer lightning storm
This land holds our fury
Growing, faster than the corn

This land's made of burial mounds
That cattle walk upon
The slowly thinning milkweed
The ghost of all that's gone

Dream: July 14

-This may or may not be about Twilight Sparkle

She was coming back after a time away, studying a magic only she could learn. No one questioned what she said, and school drama was vaporized under the phrase. "I'm a fourth level deity, and I do what I want."

It didn't stop someone from kidnapping her friends in the night just as they had the year before. She was annoyed more than anything, following the demands of this villainess with a building anger. Didn't she know this was child's play now? That it was pointless? That she would always win?

A little skunk was at the sliding door, soaking wet and she opened it, asking if it would like to towel off.

A mail carrier was standing behind it, but as soon as he was addressed he turned to a black mist and came inside.

Slinker was a shape shifter that could transform in firelight. He was a tall anthropomorphic weasel and she knew him already.

He was cruel to those who were cruel to his pet and an inconvenience to those who were not and she accepted his presence with a roll of her eyes, drying off his skunk as he prattled dramatics.

I didn't get to see how it ends, but I'm not worried about her.

Those stories always end the same way, and she always wins.

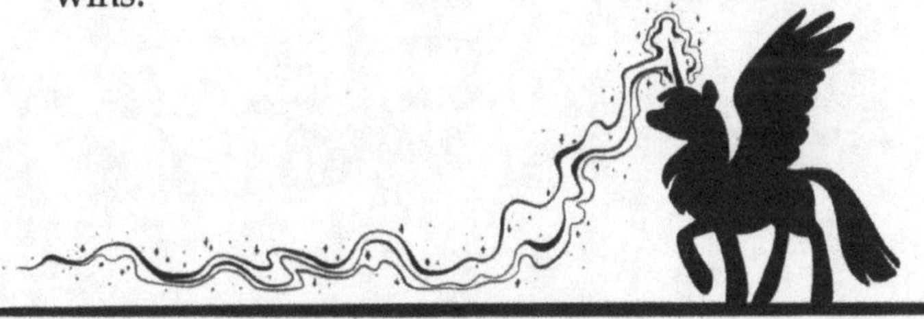

Questions and Answers
July 2021

-What can we really know?

Are we just shadows cast on a cave wall?

No, it's not that complicated.

Are we just nothing? Less than we thought?

No, it's not that simple.

We are the universe perceiving itself

The most interesting thing in billions of lightyears

And the more that we know

The more questions we grow

Were we meant to ask these questions?

And when it's too much to grasp

Go back to your past

Go back to your roots

No language, no thought,

And simply hold onto each other

It's not just the brain

That brought us through this pain

It's these wide open, grasping hands

We are the universe perceiving itself

The most interesting thing in billions of light years

And I love the stars

But they were never meant to smile

I don't know if man was meant to see the stars

But I know I was meant to hold you here close to me

Important

July 26, 2021

-I'm getting to that last part.

There lives in me a desperation to be important.

Even in writing that one line I wonder if anyone will read it, will think it clever or profound or relatable.

I almost used the word "penned" in that last sentence, but that wouldn't be accurate. It was typed, silently, as most of my unimportant thoughts, in the Notes app of my outdated iPhone.

In my writing, in my art, even in the way I arrange my things, I do it for myself, but that is hardly enough.
I cannot seem to escape this desire to please some amorphous eye that will not turn on me. (Whether it is the public, or the internet, or the "male gaze", or god)

There. Is that good? Tell me you think it's good. I won't believe you if you do but please oh please tell me somewhere there is something I did that mattered.

Even in my sorrow, in my failure.

Am I an artist now?

Am I a genius now?

Am I important now?

I only do this for me. I wish so desperately to believe myself when I say I don't care what "the other people" think.

I really don't. Not as individuals. But there is again that amorphous eye.

Maybe I didn't get enough praise as a child, maybe I'm just self-obsessed, tilting on the knife's edge of self-loathing and self-worship. Doesn't really matter in the end. Not to anyone but me. I read my poetry aloud just to see how it tastes on my tongue and it's better than food.

God, I should really get a therapist.

I Don't Self Harm
August 5, 2021

-Fiction is a balm and a sting all at once.

I don't self harm. Not really.

But I do spend too much time imagining all the things that I could have been, the feelings I could have had. And I have a good imagination, but nothing can tell me what it's really like to be held without condition. I go hunting for those romances that sting as they slide down my throat, all the hurt too real (even exaggerated as it is) and the comfort imagined.

I want it to make me happy. I want it to be enough.

I end it thinking "that was good" "what a great story" "excellent character development" and I can ride the warm and fuzzies for a minute before it crumbles. I'm always crying at the end of love stories, though only the good ones, the ones that I can believe might be able to exist. It's what makes the fantasy of it so terrible. I really don't know.

Won't someone tell me how it's supposed to feel?

I'm stuck in this half-way weep, unable to commit even to this, the lump in my throat and the tension between my brows, and those breathy, half-committed sobs like it's lodged in my throat. Somehow it feels like a performance for no one.

I don't self harm.

But I do orbit my own misery, my own desperate loneliness, my poetry a tuneless broken record.

My Own Cassandra

August 8, 2021

-Are there empty spaces here? I'll finish it someday, I will, I will.

I imagine tension in empty spaces.

Cut myself on Occam's razor.

In the place between breaths I imagine endings.

-

I am my own Cassandra.

My own heretic.

My own vengeful god.

Lullabies

August 21, 2021

-It isn't enough but it's what I'll do.

I sing myself lullabies

    Nowadays.

I buy myself toys,

I let myself indulge

In all her secret joys.

Wrap one arm around the other

And in a gentle voice

Say,

"Darling I love you. It's going to be ok."

And I sing myself lullabies,

    Nowadays.

Sweetcorn

September 11, 2021

-There are some parts of the past that I miss. I've cleansed my life of what could remind me of what I was.

I didn't have sweet corn this year.

I really wanted to.

But the thought of shucking it into the trash instead of over the fence to the goats - the sun on my back and their contended noises - the thought of getting out my big pot and only cooking maybe two or three cobs, watching them bob sadly beneath my tongs, the thought of eating them in silence - no longer watching each of our respective piles grow to the grotesque, joyous sounds of our eating, the thought of doing it all several times when I inevitably buy a dozen…I couldn't do it.

Not this year.

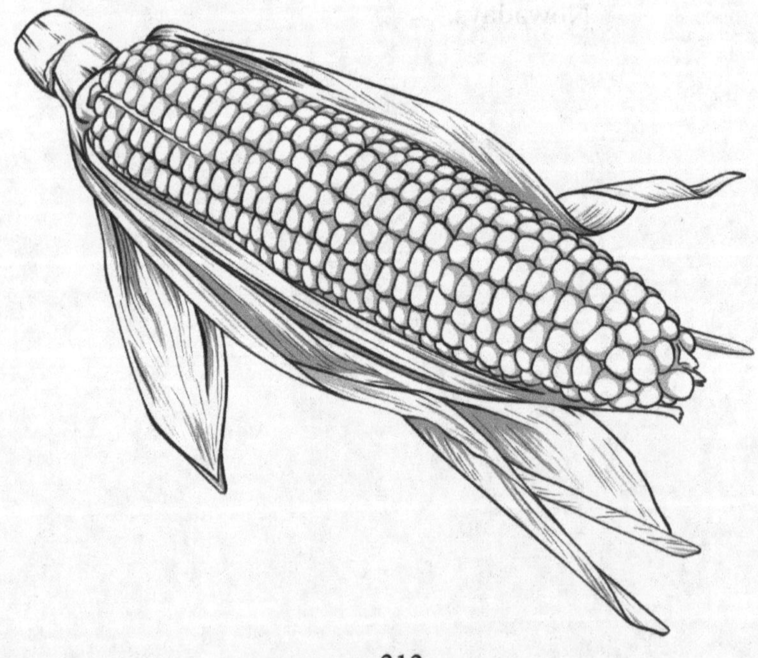

Belief

September 26, 2021

-There's mourning here, but it wasn't me who killed God

I don't believe in most of what I used to.

It's relief, and it's grief, and it's building what I thought I was from the basement up.

There's a part of me that wishes I could still believe it.

I want to go home.

A persistent thought, but I'm wishing for something that never existed the same way I find myself pleading with god - reaching with a phantom limb.

I wish I could believe there was at least some good in it, some truth in it. But leafing through the Bible feels like going through the texts of an abusive ex. There's a loss and sick attachment but I can't hold onto that anymore.

I don't believe in much of what I used to.

But I still believe in humanity, despite everything. Maybe now more than before.

We aren't fallen angels, but there's community and music woven into our DNA.

I have to believe it.

I don't believe in the system.

I don't believe in immediate solutions.

But I believe in tomorrow.

I have to.

River's Edge Inn - Dixon, IL
October 9, 2021

-I've reached some turn in the road.

We drive a lot.

Three hours, five hours, six...just to get anywhere worthwhile, to get out, to be...somewhere.

We stop a lot of places on the way from here to there, a lot of somewheres.

This somewhere feels familiar, like a doppelganger of an uncle I only sort of know. It was the only town nearby off the highway and any somewhere with food was good enough.

The roads are those tipping, "two-lane" blacktops that dip to nowhere, towards yet another little river inevitably emptying itself into the Mississippi, to be unmade in the dead gulf.

Our destination was one of those windowless wood boxes with no street appeal, a crumbling parking lot with old timers waddling forward, pretending they don't see us.

The door is tucked into the building like it's shy, like it's shielding itself from the weather.

This is just the sort of place I grew up in - the sort of nowhere that's somewhere - but these people don't know that.

There's something about returning to your roots that makes you realize just how much you've changed. (It's not a new idea, but this little restaurant is easier to swallow than listening to my family talk and realizing we don't fit together anymore, that I've changed and they won't.)

There's dark makeup on my eyes and a snake in my car, there's wisdom and strangeness on my face, there's technology at my fingertips, and I'm sure the people here would not like me much. Still, I find some kind of satisfaction in thinking of them talking about me as I leave, discussing an alien not knowing I'm one of theirs.

This place isn't particularly well put together. Ok. It's ugly. But it wouldn't have to be - and I think there's both tragedy and hope in that. One whole wall of the building is covered in windows, contrasting the dark corners on the opposite side: the sticky bar and the brightly colored neons of a few gambling machines.

This place is embarrassed of itself. It's full of cheap, anachronistic beach decor, and starfish, and anchors - beach house blue - a denial of the Midwest green in the river below, of the trees on either side.

I go to the bathroom, and the beachouse cringe continues, advertising a vacation this place could never deliver on. The stalls are made of composite wood, so overpainted with sticky pinkish-brown that the latch has been replaced. Replaced - but not removed - retired to the nowhere that is somewhere just like every old white codger in this building.

The food is still good. We knew it would be, even this nowhere is not untouched by internet reviews and pictures. But even without that, beer batter in a hell hole like this is always heaven.

The servings are generous and fried, the buns are buttered and toasted, the coleslaw is only for some, but the fries are good with anything. I could wear the onion rings as bracelets.

The onion slides out sometimes, slippery and harsh and I leave it on the plate, eat the batter and dip it in ranch - take just the good parts of my childhood - try to remember what I loved.

I'll never be back there, I'll never see those people again, but we took the onion rings with us - those will still be good tomorrow. I'll never be back there again, but I'll be somewhere similar, somewhere nowhere, somewhere sinister in its familiarity.

I've grown up, but I don't know if I'll ever grow out of it, and I'll keep the grit and the grease for myself, try to make the rest better. I'd clean those windows, get rid of the denial that it's a building on a little river and not a resort in the Keys. I would embrace the beauty that is already there.

It's what we all should do for ourselves - find the parts worth keeping, take out the trash, make yourself into something you love, something that brings you peace, but through it all - don't try to be someone you're not.

-

This is the end of the book.

This is not the end of my words.

Not yet.

Not by a long shot.

-

-